Strategic Human Resource Management

Strategic Human Resource Management

Formulating and Implementing HR Strategies for a Competitive Advantage

Ananda Das Gupta

Routledge
Taylor & Francis Group

A PRODUCTIVITY PRESS BOOK

First published 2020
by Routledge
52 Vanderbilt Avenue, New York, NY 10017
and by Routledge
2 Park Square, Milton Park, Abingdon, Oxon, OX14 4RN

Routledge is an imprint of the Taylor & Francis Group, an informa business
© 2020 Taylor & Francis

Library of Congress Cataloging-in-Publication Data

Names: Das Gupta, Ananda, 1955- author.
Title: Strategic human resource management : formulating and implementing HR strategies for a competitive advantage / Ananda Das Gupta.
Description: New York, NY : Routledge, 2020. | Includes bibliographical references and index.
Identifiers: LCCN 2019056496 (print) | LCCN 2019056497 (ebook) | ISBN 9780367345242 (hbk) | ISBN 9780429327728 (ebk)
Subjects: LCSH: Personnel management. | Strategic planning. | Organizational effectiveness.
Classification: LCC HF5549 .D35 2020 (print) | LCC HF5549 (ebook) | DDC 658.3/01--dc23
LC record available at https://lccn.loc.gov/2019056496
LC ebook record available at https://lccn.loc.gov/2019056497

ISBN: 978-0-367-34524-2 (hbk)
ISBN: 978-0-429-32772-8 (ebk)

Typeset in Garamond
by Deanta Global Publishing Services, Chennai, India

Contents

Author

Dr. Ananda Das Gupta has been engaged in teaching and research for more than twenty-five years at different universities and institutes across India. He is currently Head of the Human Resource Development and Chairperson of the Fellow (Doctoral) Programme at the Indian Institute of Plantation Management, Bangalore, a National Autonomous Institute under the Ministry of Commerce, Government of India. He also serves as an Adjunct Professor at the Indian Institute of Management, Kozhikode, and the Indian Institute of Management, Rohtak. He has also been the Mentor Faculty at Indian Institute of Management Sirmaur.

Dr. Das Gupta did his doctorate as a UGC Research Fellow. He has published many papers in various refereed journals and has four books to his credit in the areas of organizational development, strategic human resources management, corporate social responsibility and business ethics. He is currently Editor-in-Chief of the *International Journal of Business Ethics in Developing Economies*, and serves on the Editorial Boards of leading international journals. He is also on the International Editorial Board for *Encyclopaedia on Corporate Social Responsibility*, published in five volumes by Springer.

He has been the Project Director of ICSSR (Indian Council of Social Science Research) and was the National Co-Ordinator: Tea Productivity Council of India, sponsored by the government of India

In addition, he has long been associated with IJSE as a reviewer and as a Guest Editor for the Special Issue on India of *International Journal of Social Economics*, Emerald Group, England, 2008.

His areas of research interests are: social justice; inequality; disability; poverty, labour; employment; trade unions; income; wages; industrial relations, common good; community; social capital; citizenship; civil society, ethical and moral theory; social philosophy, voluntary associations; NGOs; social movements and environmental economics and ethics; and sustainable development.

Chapter 1

Introduction to Strategic Human Resource Management

Introduction

The origin of the concept of Strategic Human Resource Management (SHRM) can be traced back to the military system – to the Greek word "strategos," which means a general who organizes, leads and directs his forces to the most advantageous position. In the world of business, it mainly denotes how top management leads the organization in a particular direction in order to achieve its specific goals, objectives, vision and overall purpose in the society in a given context/ environment. The main emphasis of strategy is thus to enable an organization to achieve a competitive advantage with its unique capabilities by focusing on the present and future directions of the organization.

Learning Objectives

Three central arguments are made in this introductory chapter.

(1) That a growing body of evidence converges to suggest that the changes taking place in the global business environment are often not accompanied by complementary changes in Human Resource Management practices, thereby leading to a situation in which the failure of some firms is due to the mismanagement of people rather than to problems with the technical systems per se.

(2) That this is because organizations have achieved relatively low levels of effectiveness in implementing SHRM practices (Huselid et al., 1997), especially in emerging economies of Southeast Asia and other developing countries like Nigeria, which are exposed to the challenges and opportunities of globalization.

(3) That in order to manage employees to achieve the competitive edge in a period of globalization, human resource personnel must possess relevant competencies for implementing such SHRM policies and practices (Barney and Wright, 1988; Huselid et al., 1997; Ulrich and Yeung, 1989, 1996; Ulrich et al., 1995).

I

Developments in the field of Human Resource Management (HRM) are now well documented in the management literature. The roots of HRM go back as far as the 1950s, when writers like Drucker and McGregor stressed the need for visionary goal-directed leadership and the management of business integration. The "configurational" perspective posits a simultaneous internal and external fit between a firm's external environment, business strategy and HR strategy, implying that business strategies and HRM policies interact, according to the organizational context, in determining business performance.

Mintzberg (1987) says that a formal approach to devising a strategy results in deliberation on the part of the decision-makers, which results in thinking before action. On the other hand, the incremental approach allows the strategy to emerge in response to an evolving situation. Lundy and Cowling (1996: 23), summarizing Mintzberg's thinking, write that deliberate strategy precludes learning, while emergent strategy fosters it but precludes control. Effective strategies combine deliberation and control with flexibility and organizational learning. A number of scholars have criticized Mintzberg's work as over-prescriptive.

Organizations adopting the classical approach (like the army) follow a clear, rational, planned and deliberate process of strategy formation and aim for maximization of profits. This approach is most likely to be successful when the organization's objectives and goals are clear, the external environment is relatively stable, the information about both the external and internal environments is reliable, and the decision-makers are able to analyze the strategy thoroughly and make highly calculated decisions in order to adopt the best possible choice. Strategy formulation is undertaken by top managers, and the implementation is carried out by operational managers of different departments.

Lengnick-Hall and Lengnick-Hall (1999: 29–30) summarize a variety of topics that have been the focus of SHRM writers over the past couple of decades. These include HR accounting (which attempts to assign a value to human resources in an effort to quantify organizational capacity), HR planning, responses of HRM to strategic changes in the business environment, matching human resources to strategic or organizational conditions and the broader scope of HR strategies. For these writers, SHRM is a multidimensional process with multiple effects. Such writing also highlights the growing proactive nature of the HR function, its increased potential contribution to the success of organizations and the mutual relationships (integration) between business strategy and HRM.

Fombrun et al.'s (1984) "matching model" highlights the "resource" aspect of HRM and emphasizes the efficient utilization of human resources to meet organizational objectives. This means that, like other resources of the organization, human resources have to be obtained at low cost, used sparingly and developed and exploited as fully as possible. The matching model is mainly based on Chandler's (1962) argument that an organization's structure is an outcome of its strategy. Fombrun et al. (1984) expanded this premise in their model of SHRM, which emphasizes a "tight fit" between organizational strategy, organizational structure and the HRM system. The organizational strategy is pre-eminent; both the organizational structure and HRM are dependent on the organization's strategy. The main aim of the matching model is therefore to develop an appropriate "human resource system" that will characterize those HRM strategies that contribute to the most efficient implementation of business strategies.

In recent decades, researchers have given due recognition to the theories and literature regarding SHRM. Strong and comprehensive theoretical frameworks help in concentrating and consolidating research efforts, which facilitates the conversion of HRM practices into real strategic standards. SHRM is based on two principles. First is the belief that the organization's human resources are of vital strategic importance. This means that every employee's personal traits, talent, behavior and interactions are potentially important in the formulation of basic strategies and, more importantly, putting these strategies into practice. Second is the idea that HRM practices should be utilized in order to increase the strategic strength of the organization. Appropriate methods of HRM play an important role in the strategic success of organizations. Wright and McMahan (1992) defined Strategic Human Resource Management as "the pattern of planned human resource deployments and activities intended to enable the firm to achieve its goals" (p. 298). In 1980, a strategic approach to human resources was emphasized by many scholars. Changes in thinking and practice caused an increase in specialization, and thus it led to decreased use of the term "personnel management" in Human Resource Management. In the 1980s and 1990s, changes in the operational environment of HRM drew attention to the strategic management of human resources. According to studies done by many researchers, for instance, Mabey et al. (1998), one of the most important issues in the 1980s, which developed SHRM, was the industrial crisis in the United States. This led to major changes in personnel management, and the focus on the strategic management of human resources increased.

Three different patterns of assumptions emerged during the 1990s, and Delery and Doty (1996) provided a useful scheme for categorizing these major SHRM theoretical perspectives. The universal perspective argues that some HR practices have a positive effect on organizational performance across all organizations and under all conditions. Which HR practices are universal has remained a source of debate. Essentially, this position argues that there is no need to fit HR practices into a particular strategy or in a particular organizational context. The configurational perspective argues that unique patterns of HR practices have a positive effect on organizational performance. Additionally, the assumption of equifinality means that more than one configuration may be effective in any given setting. Using a stratified sample of 1050 banks, Delery and Doty (1996) found relatively strong support for the universalistic perspective as well as some support for both the contingency and configurational perspectives. Youndt, Snell, Dean and Lepak (1996) compared the universalistic perspective with the contingency perspective of SHRM in a study conducted using a sample of 97 plants in a manufacturing setting. The results supported the contingency approach.

They found that an HR system focused on human capital enhancement in organizations pursuing a quality enhancement strategy related to multiple dimensions of operational performance. The researchers argued that a universalistic and a contingency perspective are not necessarily mutually exclusive – an assertion that others have also made. In other words, universal "best practices" provide a solid foundation of SHRM activities, but to achieve a higher level of performance, contingent factors should be considered. Boxall and Purcell (2000) weighed in on the debate between best fit (i.e., the contingency perspective) and best practices (i.e., the universalistic perspective). They concluded that there is little evidence to support the universalistic perspective. However, they encouraged a broader view on the contingency theory than had been examined previously. Additionally, they argued that the resource-based view of the firm had been useful in SHRM research and encouraged researchers to investigate how HR activities could influence knowledge creation and organizational renewal. Using a sample of 286 Japanese affiliates operating in mainland China and Taiwan, Takeuchi, Wakabayashi and Chen (2003) found support for a configurational hypothesis (i.e., that each HRM technique could be used in a way that is symmetrical to the process of enlarging the capacity of corporate organizational learning), predicting the financial outcomes of an affiliate's performance. Chang and Huang (2005) also tested the universalistic and contingency approaches to SHRM using a sample of 235 Taiwanese firms. They found no support for the universalistic perspective, but they found that an innovative product market strategy did moderate the relationship between HR practices and organizational performance.

In recent years, SHRM has been very useful in developed countries. According to research, more than half of the organizations in these countries, by using the results of the predefined strategies, could achieve new capabilities in their SHRM practices. Fambrun and his colleagues believed that the human resource systems and organizational structures must be managed in such a way that they are consistent and compatible with the organizational strategies. Miller argues that HR strategies should be integrated with corporate strategies. For this integration, the management measures in the field of human resources should be coordinated and synchronized with other areas of the organization's activities.

A number of researchers studying the interaction of organizations' systems and Human Resource Management have found that SHRM, by creating harmony between organizational strategies and HR policies, bring synergy to the activities of an organization. Many HR researchers believe that the HR department should have a greater role in strategy formulation and the organization of forces. HR systems should strive to be harmonious with the overall strategies of the organization.

In developing countries, applying the models of HR strategy is not given due consideration. Few studies have examined the importance of SHRM and its impact on the overall organizational success in Malaysia. The main reasons are the newly emerged concept of SHRM, relevant knowledge, the lack of maturation of strategic dialogue in this area, the lack of resources and references in native languages and the lack of attention to the localization of successful and innovative international models. The matrix of SWOT analysis is an important tool through which managers can compare the information and provide four types of strategies. Comparison of the internal and external key elements of this matrix is the most important part as it requires precise judgment.

Despite the many criticisms, however, the matching model deserves credit for providing an initial framework for subsequent theory development in the field of SHRM. Researchers need to adopt a comprehensive methodology in order to study the dynamic concept of human resource strategy. Do elements of the matching model exist in different settings? This can be discovered by examining the presence of some of the core issues of the model. The main propositions emerging from the matching models that can be adopted by managers to evaluate the scenario of SHRM in their organizations are:

Do organizations show a "tight fit" between their HRM practices and organizational strategy where the former is dependent on the latter? Do specialist people managers believe they should develop HRM systems only for the effective implementation of their organization's strategies? Do organizations consider their human resources as a cost and use them sparingly? Or do they devote resources to the training of their HRs to make the best use of them? Do HRM strategies vary across different levels of employees?

SHRM therefore has many different components, including HR policies, culture, values and practices. Schuler (1992) developed a "5-P model" of SHRM that melds 5 HR activities (philosophies, policies, programs, practices and processes) with strategic business needs and reflects the management's overall plan for survival, growth, adaptability and profitability. Strategic HR activities form the main components of HR strategy. This model to a great extent explains the significance of these 5 SHRM activities in achieving the organization's strategic needs and shows the interrelatedness of activities that are often treated separately in the literature. This is helpful in understanding the complex interaction between organizational strategy and SHRM activities.

Michael Porter (1980; 1985) identified three possible generic strategies for competitive advantage in business: cost leadership (when the organization cuts its prices by producing a product or service at less expense than its competitors), innovation (when the organization is able to be a unique producer) and quality (when the organization is delivering high-quality goods and services to customers). Considering the emphasis on "external fit" (i.e., organizational strategy leading individual HR practices that interact with the organizational strategy in order to improve organizational performance), a number of HRM combinations can be adopted by firms to support Porter's model of business strategies.

Strategic human resource planning is a crucial factor in the fulfillment of the fundamental strategic objectives of any organization. It is based on the idea that human resources are the most important strategic resource considered inside the organization. Any human resources strategy sets out to achieve a number of objectives and seeks to prove the efficiency of its programs. Specialists in human resources make a distinction between "hard" and "soft" human resource planning.

The former is based on quantitative analysis in order to ensure that the right number of the right qualified sort of people is available when needed. "Soft" human resource planning is more explicitly focused on creating and shaping the culture of the organization so that there is a clear integration between corporate goals and employee values, beliefs and behaviors. But, as it is pointed out, the soft version becomes virtually synonymous with the whole subject of Human Resource Management.

In order to design a SWOT matrix, the following 8 steps must be completed:

1) Prepare a list of major opportunities of the organization's external environment.
2) Prepare a list of major threats of the organization's external environment.
3) Prepare a list of major strengths of the organization's internal environment.
4) Prepare a list of major weaknesses of the organization's internal environment.
5) Compare internal strengths with external opportunities and enter the result under the SO strategies.
6) Compare internal weaknesses with external opportunities and enter the results under the WO strategies.
7) Compare the internal strengths with external threats and enter the results under the ST strategies.
8) Reduce internal weaknesses and avoid external threats.

The purpose of the PEST analysis is to study the environmental factors including political, economic, social and technological. This evaluation helps in identifying the factors of the SWOT analysis, thus leading to a transparent understanding of the environmental condition of the organization.

Strategic human resource planning must rely on the global strategic analysis of the organization and take into account the demographical changes. When calculating the needs of human resources, we analyze real data supplied by plans based on the outcome of the following interrelated planning activities (Armstrong, 2006):

Demand forecasting – estimating the future needs for people and competencies with reference to corporate and functional plans and forecasts of future activity levels.

Supply forecasting – estimating the supply of people with reference to the analyses of current resources and future availability. The forecast will also take account of labor market trends relating to the availability of skills and to demographics.

Action planning – preparing plans to deal with forecast deficit through internal promotion, training or external recruitment, retention strategies and different changes in the process of motivating the workforce, increasing flexibility, etc. The literature in the domain describes a series of methods to determine the human resources needed in an organization. This depends on the volume and the structure of the activity that will be developed and also on external factors such as changes in the economic branch, competition, customers, etc. One of the most developed methods used to determine the human resource requirements is the Regressive method. It establishes certain relations between employees, regarding their quantitative and qualitative features, and provides some indicators of the activity of the company, such as the sales volume, the production volume, added value, etc.

The human resources required are estimated based on these relations, taking into account the values of the indicators planned by the organization. This is a method that cannot take into consideration future information about the competition, new technologies, demand forecasting, etc., and this limits the accuracy of the forecasting. Trend analysis is the method by which human resources forecasting is based on the previous years' evolution of the number of employees and their structure. Forecasts of what human resources will be needed are made by every line manager. This method supposes that at the level of each work department or production section, the line managers should be able to evaluate the future needs of employees in relation to the volume and the specificity of the activity. These estimations must be correlated with the overall strategy of the organization. The Delphi method is especially used in a company in which it is hard to quantify the estimations of the volume of future activities. It is organized by a group of 10–20 specialists who know very well the object of the developed activity.

The experts make statements about the future development of the organization and fill a number of questionnaires during multiple sessions coordinated by an expert in economic forecasting. The purpose is to reach an agreement on future estimations regarding the overall activity of the company and the human resource requirement. The coordinator synthesizes the estimations made by the experts and asks for explanations for each of their answers that deviate from the average. Generally, after 3 or 5 stages of questioning, the specialists reach a consensus. The whole process ends with a discussion between the specialists about the human resources forecasting.

The shift to an emphasis on human capital contribution was firmly established by Wright and McMahan (1992) who developed a definition of SHRM that has become widely accepted over the years. They defined it simply as "the pattern of planned human resource deployments and activities intended to enable an organization to achieve its goals" (p. 298). In this article, they identified six theoretical models of SHRM: the behavioral perspective, cybernetic models, agency/ transaction cost theory, the resource-based view of the firm, power/resource dependence models and institutional theory. This article appeared at a time when the SHRM literature was evolving in a largely disjointed and a theoretical fashion. Following its publication, more attention was paid to building SHRM theory on the foundation of established theories from other fields.

Human capital is a key source of innovation and competitive improvement. Exploiting its potential and boosting its value to the organization involves a systematic process to determine the competencies that are fundamental to achieve enhanced job performance. However, why do organizations often fail to successfully cope with the main challenges of the knowledge and learning society and to identify the consequences for learning technologies? This chapter discusses a holistic model for human resource management strategy required to technologically support the organization toward a forceful and comprehensive solution. By applying a stepwise approach, the components that organizations should consider are identified, along with their interrelationships, and the increased need for a harmonizing worldwide standardization in this field of application.

Organizations must increasingly demonstrate, with data, that their human resource strategies significantly enhance competitive advantage, not simply that they are efficient or "best-in-class." This unprecedented attention to human capital has been matched by an explosion of human capital data and measurement approaches. HR information systems accelerate the trend, continually lowering the cost and increasing the speed of data storage and delivery. It is now quite feasible to obtain hundreds of human capital measures in the blink of an eye and to conduct equally dizzying "cuts" and trends.

It is common to assess HR customer satisfaction by asking key decision-makers if they like the HR measures or if the HR measures seem "businesslike." Yet, it would seem rather ludicrous to assess the financial analysis framework by asking whether business leaders liked it (in fact, if they miss their numbers, they hate it!).

The financial decision system is so logically connected to key organizational outcomes, and so able to enhance important decisions about financial resources, that it is accepted even when its message is unpleasant. So, the key consideration in any human capital measurement system is its ability to enhance decisions by articulating the logical connection between talent and organizational outcomes. Measurement is an essential building block of such a decision-making framework. In finance, rich bond rating systems enable financial theorists to develop a portfolio theory, to guide decisions about the risk and return of sets of securities. So, the explosion of HR measures is a necessary condition for developing talent, but today's measures often lack a logical framework that articulates the key connections between talent decisions and organizational strategic success.

The 21st century began with earthshaking events that have irreversibly reshaped the role of corporations, governments and the employment relationship. We are entering an era where measuring profits, shareholder value or even competitive success is insufficient. Emotions, global diversity, values, affiliation, significance, balance, meaning and integrity are increasingly prominent organizational goals. Organizational leaders will increasingly be expected to provide greater transparency regarding the logic of their decisions. Accounting scandals such as Enron didn't occur because the numbers weren't there, but because analysts could not or did not hold decision-makers accountable to explain the connection between the measures, key business processes and the shareholder value.

II

SHRM involves a set of internally consistent policies and practices designed and implemented to ensure that a firm's human capital (employees) contributes to the achievement of its business objectives (Baird and Meshoulam, 1988; Delery and Doty, 1996; Huselid et al., 1997; Jackson and Schuler, 1995). Schuler (1992: 18) has developed a more comprehensive academic definition of SHRM:

> Strategic human resources management is largely about integration and adaptation. Its concern is to ensure that (1) human resources (HR) management is fully integrated with the strategy and the strategic needs of the firm; (2) HR policies cohere both across policy areas and across hierarchies; and (3) HR practices are adjusted, accepted and used by line managers and employees as part of their everyday work.

For Wright and McMahan (1992), SHRM refers to "the pattern of planned human resource deployments and activities intended to enable an organization to achieve its goals" (p. 298). To sum up, it appears that some of the frequently cited fundamental elements of SHRM in the literature are: SHRM practices are macro-oriented, proactive and long-term focused in nature; SHRM views human resources as assets or investments, not expenses; the implementation of SHRM practices is linked to organizational performance; and focusing on the alignment of human resources with the firm's strategy is a means of gaining a competitive advantage (Nee and Khatri, 1999: 311).

Theoretical Foundations of SHRM

Several theoretical perspectives have been developed to classify the ways in which HR practices are impacted by strategic considerations, which are briefly described below. Wright and

McMahan (1992) have developed a comprehensive theoretical framework consisting of six theoretical influences. Four of these influences provide explanations on practices resulting from strategy considerations. These include, among others, the resource-based view of the firm and the behavioral view. The other two theories provide explanations on HR practices that are not driven by strategy considerations: (1) resource dependence and (2) institutional theory.

The resource-based theory of the firm blends concepts from organizational economics and strategic management (Barney, 1991). This theory holds that a firm's resources are key determinants of its competitive advantage. Firms can develop this competitive advantage only by creating value in a way that is difficult for competitors to imitate. Traditional sources that provide a competitive advantage, such as financial and natural resources, technology and economies of scale, can be used to create value. However, the resource-based argument is that these sources are increasingly accessible and easy to imitate. Thus they are less significant for gaining a competitive advantage especially in comparison with a complex social structure such as an employment system. If that is so, human resource policies and practices may be an important source of a sustained competitive advantage (Jackson and Schuler, 1995; Pfeffer, 1994). Specifically, four empirical indicators of the potential of a firm's resources to generate a competitive advantage are value, rareness, imitability and substitutability (Barney, 1991). In other words, to gain a competitive advantage, the resources available to competing firms must be variable among competitors, and these resources must be rare (not easily obtained). Three types of resources associated with organizations are (a) physical (plant, technology and equipment geographic location); (b) human (employees' experience and knowledge); (c) organizational (structure, systems for planning, monitoring and controlling activities; social relations within the organization and between the organization and external constituencies). HR practices greatly influence an organization's human and organizational resources and so can be used to gain competitive advantages (Schuler and MacMillan, 1984).

The second theoretical influence is the behavioral view, which is based on the contingency theory. This view explains the practices designed to control and influence attitudes and behaviors and stresses the instrumentality of such practices in achieving strategic objectives. The cybernetic system explains the adoption or abandonment of HR practices on the basis of feedback on execution or enforcement of a strategy. For example, training programs may be adopted to help pursue a strategy and would subsequently be adopted or abandoned based on feedback. The fourth influence, based on transaction costs, explains why organizations use control systems such as performance evaluation and reward systems. The argument is that in the absence of performance evaluation systems that are linked to reward systems, strategies might not be pursued. The other two theories provide explanations on HR practices that are not driven by strategy considerations but are based on power and political influences, control of resources (resource-based theory) and expectations of social responsibility (institutional theory) (Greer, 1995: 107–108).

Implications of HRM Practices

The idea that individual HR practices impacts on performance in an additive fashion (Delery and Doty, 1996) is inconsistent with the emphasis on internal fit in the resource-based view of the firm. With its implicit systems perspective, the resource-based view suggests the importance of "complementary resources," the notion that individual policies or practices "have limited ability to generate competitive advantage". This idea that a system of HR practices may be more than the sum of the parts appears to be consistent with discussions on synergy, configurations, contingency factors, external and internal fit, holistic approach, etc. (Delery and Doty, 1996; Huselid, 1995). Drawing on the theoretical works of Osterman (1987), Sonnenfeld and Peiperl (1988),

Kerr and Slocum (1987) and Miles and Snow (1984), Delery and Doty (1996) identified seven practices that are consistently considered strategic HR practices. These are (1) internal career opportunity, (2) formal training systems, (3) appraisal measures, (4) profit sharing, (5) employment security, (6) voice mechanisms and (7) job definition. There are other SHRM practices that might affect organizational performance. For example, Schuler and Jackson (1987) presented a very comprehensive list of HR practices. However, the seven practices listed by Delery and Doty appear to have the greatest support across a diverse literature. For example, nearly all of these are among Pfeffer's (1994) 16 most effective practices for managing people.

An obvious question at this juncture is: how can organizations effectively adopt, implement and maximize HRM practices for value-added firm-level outcomes? That is, how can firms increase the probability that they will adopt and then effectively implement appropriate HRM practices? Ensuring that members of the HRM team have the appropriate human capital or competencies has been suggested as one way to increase the likelihood of effective implementation of HRM practices (Huselid et al., 1997).

Ulrich and Yeung (1989) argue that HR professionals in the future will need four basic competencies to become partners in the strategic management process. These include business competency, professional and technical knowledge, integration competence and the ability to manage change.

On the other hand, the UK-based Management Charter Initiative (MCI), an independent competence-based management development organization, identifies 7 key roles and required competencies. These include competencies required to handle roles like managing activities, managing resources, managing people, managing information, managing energy, managing quality and managing projects (MCI Management Standards, April, 1997). Finally, Huselid et al. (1997) identified two sets of competencies as important for HR personnel: (1) HR professional competencies and (2) business-related competencies.

HR professional competence describes the state-of-the-art HR knowledge, expertise and skill relevant for performing excellently within a traditional HR functional department such as recruitment and selection, training, compensation, etc. This competence ensures that technical HR knowledge is both present and used within a firm (Huselid et al., 1997). Business-related competence refers to the amount of business experience HR personnel have had outside the functional HR specialty. These capabilities should facilitate the selection and implementation of HRM policies and practices that fit the unique characteristics of a firm including its size, strategy, structure and culture (Jackson and Schuler, 1995). In other words, these competencies will enable the HR staff to know the company's business and understand the economic and financial capabilities necessary for making logical decisions that support the company's strategic plan based on the most accurate information possible.

III

SHRM and Organizational Performance

Researchers in SHRM posit that greater use of such practices will always result in better (or worse) organizational performance (Abowd, 1990; Gerhart and Milkovich, 1990; Huselid, 1995; Leonard, 1990; Terpstra and Rozell, 1993). Leonard (1990) found that organizations having long-term incentive plans for their executives had larger increases in return on equity over a 4-year period than did other organizations. Abowd (1990) found that the degree to which managerial compensation was based on an organization's financial performance was significantly related to future financial performance. Gerhart and Milkovich (1990) found that pay mix was related to financial performance. Organizations with pay plans that included a greater amount of performance contingent pay achieved superior financial performance. In combination, these studies indicate that organizations with stronger pay-for-performance norms achieved better long-term financial performance than did organizations with weaker pay-for-performance norms.

Terpstra and Rozell (1993) posited 5 "best" staffing practices and found that the use of these practices had a moderate and positive relationship with organizational performance. Finally, Huselid (1995) identified a link between organization-level outcomes and groups of high-performance work practices. Instead of focusing on a single practice (e.g., staffing), Huselid assessed the simultaneous use of multiple sophisticated HR practices and concluded that the HR sophistication of an organization was significantly related to turnover, organizational productivity and financial performance.

In the case of mandatory competencies required for HR personnel, emerging evidence from empirical research demonstrates the increasing need for HR personnel to have both HR professional and business-related skills and competencies. A survey of HR executives in the United States show that HR managers are spending relatively less time in record keeping and auditing, while their time spent on their activities as a business partner has doubled. The survey also revealed that HR managers believe that their HR staff's most important skill needs are team skills, consultation skills and an understanding of business (Noe et al., 1997).

Managerial competencies, particularly in the HR function, bring two advantages to HRM: (1) They enhance the status of the HR department (Barney and Wright, 1988) and (2) act as important influences on the level of integration between HR management and organizational strategy (Golden and Ramanujam, 1985; Ropo, 1993). A study of Singaporean companies found that when HR managers lack the necessary skills to perform their duties competently, line managers and executives take over some of the functions of HR managers (Nee and Khatri, 1999).

Research by Ropo (1993: 51) on managerial competencies stressed that "the internal dynamism of the HR function serves as the most critical mechanism to keep the integration process going after it has been started under favorable organizational and strategic circumstances." Other studies show that if HR managers can evaluate their priorities and acquire new sets of professional and personal competencies, the HR function would be able to ride the wave of business evolution proudly with other functions in the organization (Ulrich et al., 1995).

Huselid et al. (1997) conducted an elaborate study on 293 firms in the United States to evaluate the impact of human resource managers' professional/technical competencies on HR practices and the latter's impact on organizational performance. The results of the study suggest that consistent with the resource-based view of the firm, there exists a significant relationship between SHRM practices and firm performance.

They found that (1) HR-related competencies and, to a lesser extent, business-related competencies increase the extent of effective implementation of SHRM practices and (2), consistent with recent studies linking HRM activities and firm performance (Arthur, 1994; Cutcher-Gershenfeld, 1991; Huselid, 1995; Huselid and Becker, 1996; MacDuffie, 1995), investments in human resources are a potential source of competitive advantage. Recent reviews of theoretical and empirical literature (Juhary Ali and Bawa, 1999; Irwin et al., 1998; Jackson and Schuler, 1995) suggest that a variety of factors affect the relationship between HRM and firm performance. These factors include firm size, technology and union coverage.

The influence of firm size on HRM practices is fully documented in theoretical and empirical studies. For example, institutional theory suggests that larger organizations should adopt more sophisticated and socially responsive HRM practices because they are more visible and are under more pressure to gain legitimacy. Many empirical studies show that firm size is an important variable influencing HRM practices (Ng and Maki, 1993; Wagar, 1998).

There is emerging evidence that HR practices may differ in organizations depending on the level of technological sophistication in terms of training (Majchrzak, 1988), performance appraisal (Ouchi, 1977) and reward systems (Snell and Dean, 1992). Theoretical and empirical studies also support the position that the presence of specific HRM practices may differ based on the union coverage of a firm (Ng and Maki, 1993; Wagar, 1998; Lawler and Mohrman 1987).

From the discussions so far, the following issues emerge. (1) There appears to be a significant relationship between strategic HRM practices and firm performance (low employee turnover, high productivity and high profitability) (Huselid et al., 1997). (2) It is also clear that there exists low incidence of implementing SHRM practices relative to technical HRM practices (Huselid et al., 1997; Wright and McMahan, 1992). (3) Furthermore, although there exists a significant relationship between the extent of both HR professional and business-related managerial competencies and the incidence of implementing HRM practices, organizations have achieved higher levels of HR professional competencies relative to business-related competencies. (4) Finally, variables based on the environmental context such as firm size, technology and union status affect the extent of implementing HRM practices (Jackson and Schuler, 1995; Snell and Dean, 1992; Wagar, 1998). The relationships discussed above are presented in Figure 1.1 and relevant propositions are derived. This

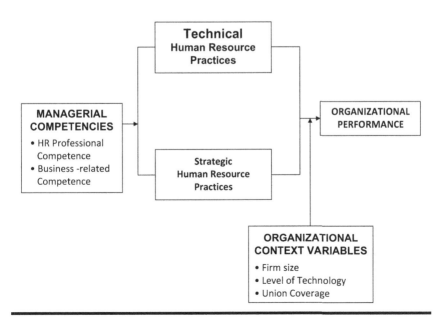

Figure 1.1   Moderating variables.

theoretical framework is in keeping with the thinking of a number of authors including Delery and Doty (1996), Huselid et al. (1997), Jackson and Schuler (1995) and Wright and McMahan (1992).

Case Study of Strategic Human Resource Management in Walmart Stores

Introduction

Sam Walton established Walmart in 1962 on 3 revolutionary philosophies: respect for the individual, service to our customers and strive for excellence. Walmart, Inc. is not only the largest discounted retailer in the world, it also ranks as the largest corporation in the world. The retail giant dwarfs its nearest competition, generating 3 times the revenues of the world's number two retailer, France's Carrefour SA. Domestically, Walmart has more than 1.2 million workers, making it the nation's largest nongovernmental employer. US operations include 1,478 Walmart discount stores (located in all 50 states). Its international operations commenced in 1991 covering Canada and Puerto Rico, including Walmart Supercenters in Argentina, Brazil, China, Germany, Mexico, Puerto Rico, South Korea and the United Kingdom (http://www.referenceforbusiness.com/history2/20/Wal-Mart-Stores-Inc.html#ixzz56lss8VII).

Walmart strives to maintain its competitive advantage through its satellite-based distribution system and by keeping store location costs to a minimum by placing stores on low-cost land outside small- to medium-sized towns, both in the United States and in its overseas affiliations.

Corporate Strategy and HR Strategy at Walmart

Walmart purchased massive quantities of items from its suppliers to form a scale economy, and its efficient stock control system helped in making its operating costs lower than those of its competitors. It also imported many goods from China, "the world's factory," for their low cost.

Managers engage in three levels of strategic planning: the corporate-level strategy; the business-level strategy and the function-level strategy. The functional strategy should serve the overall company strategy so that the corporate strategy could be implemented more effectively and efficiently.

The basic premise underlying SHRM is that organizations adopting a particular strategy require HR practices that are different from those required by organizations adopting alternative strategies (Jackson and Schuler, 1995). Generally, there are two primary SHRM theoretical models: the universalistic best practices and the contingency perspective of "best fit." The contingency perspective of "best fit" elucidates that individual HR practices will be selected based on the contingency of the specific context of a company. Walmart has different corporate strategies with those retailers with a differentiation strategy, and this enables Walmart to actually cultivate the primary contingency factor described in the SHRM literature. What's more, we should remember that individual HR practices will interact with the firm's strategy to result in organizational performance, and these interaction effects which make up the "universal best practices" of the firm may not apply so well in another company.

In the following paragraphs we'll examine the "fitness" of HR practices in Walmart against this theoretical model, which is also the integration process of HR practices with the contingency variables to some extent.

With regard to recruitment, for example, *The New York Times* (January 2004) reported on an internal Walmart audit which found "extensive violations of child-labor laws and state regulations requiring time for breaks and meals." The cheap cost of child labor and the employment of minors enable Walmart to earn a more cost-competitive advantage over other companies. Walmart has also faced a barrage of lawsuits alleging that the company discriminates against workers with disabilities, for the recruitment of these people means providing more facilities for them and the loss of efficiency to some extent.

From the training perspective, through training on the behavioral requirements for success and encouragement, Walmart tried to adjust employee behaviors and competencies to what the company's strategy required, which is to lower the cost more. This logic is also embodied in its "lock-in" of the nighttime shift in various stores. Through this enforced policy, Walmart tried to prevent "shrinkage" behavior of its employees to eliminate unauthorized cigarette breaks or quick trips home.

From the performance management perspective, Walmart made highly demanding standards and job designs. *The New York Times* reported that Walmart resorted to extensive violations of state regulations requiring time for breaks and meals. There are so many instances of minors working too late, during school hours, or for too many hours in a day, because the performance appraising just forces them to do so. In career management also, Walmart goes to great lengths to reduce cost, and there are many cases in which women sued Walmart for its policy that discriminated against women by systematically denying them promotions and paying them less than men. Women are pushed into "female" departments, and are demoted if they complain about unequal treatment, just to enable more cost reduction against its competitors.

From the compensation management perspective, Walmart has also implemented very aggressive HR policies and activities. Walmart imported $15 billion worth of goods from China, not only for the strategic consideration of the supplier chain economy, but also because Walmart has some factories in China, whose products are branded with the Walmart name. Through this method, Walmart pays much less to the Chinese laborers in this "world factory" and earns some benefits, and so we can see how Walmart's corporate strategy is intensely integrated with its HR policy. In 2002, operating costs for Walmart were just 16.6% of total sales, compared to a 20.7% average for the retail industry as a whole, which supported the overall strategy greatly. Walmart workers in California earn on average 31% less than workers employed in other large retail businesses. Actually, with other operating and inventory costs fixed by the higher level management, store managers must turn to wages to increase profits, and Walmart expects labor costs to be cut by two-tenths of a percentage point each year.

From the employee benefit and safety perspective, workers eligible for benefits such as health insurance must pay over the odds for them. In 1999, employees paid 36% of the costs. In 2001, the employee burden rose to 42%. While employees of large firms in the United States pay on average 16% of the premium for health insurance, unionized supermarket workers typically pay nothing. Walmart was frequently accused of not providing employees with affordable access to health care, but the top managers and HR managers knew that their focus was just to try their most to implement Walmart's corporate strategy.

Finally, from the labor relations perspective, Sam Walton sought to bring great value to customers through aggressive discounting. Because unionized supermarket workers typically pay nothing, Walmart has a strong anti-union policy. Allegations of firing workers sympathetic to labor organizations have been made, and all new employees are shown a propaganda videotape, that says that joining a union would have bad implications for them and that the employees should never sign a union card. In the United Kingdom it was reported in *The Guardian* that Walmart is facing the prospect of a bruising legal battle with the GMB trade union in a row over collective bargaining rights as the union would not accept Walmart withdrawing a 10% pay offer to more than 700 workers after they rejected a new package of terms and conditions, which included giving up rights to collective pay bargaining. Here there may be some doubt as to why Walmart has recently allowed unionization in their stores in China, where unionization is mandatory. However, this mandatory rule was made a long time before Walmart's walk into China, and that is why Walmart gave up its persistence in not having some unions, and its former reason to the Chinese government was that it did not have any unions in its global business. So how do we see Walmart's compromise if that constitutes a "compromise"?

It has been argued that doing business in China is particularly difficult because of the higher relative importance of personal relationships (guanxi), as opposed to the specification and enforcement of contracts in the West. Walmart China has tried every effort to develop good relationships with the Chinese government and other influential groups. So, Walmart's exception of allowing unionizations is just in accordance with its corporate strategy and HR strategy. If it ignores the Chinese government's firm rule, its cost would just outweigh what it would save by organizing no unions in its labor relations management as Walmart provides little power for Chinese workers as the unions are controlled by the state.

Conclusion

Therefore, from the above discussion we know that Human Resource Management is of strategic importance to Walmart. Both the top managers and HR executives should pay more attention to employee management on a daily basis. They should play more positive roles in training and utilizing their human resources as well as cultivating a better organizational culture, all of which may prove to be more cost effective, and correspondingly help realize Sam Walton's simple philosophy of "bringing more value to customers."

References

Abowd, J. M. 1990. Does performance-based compensation affect corporate performance? *Industrial and Labor Relations Review*, 43: 52–73.
Ali, Juhary & Bawa, M. A. 1999. Human resource management in the context of labor market and union status: A review. In: Daing Nasir Ibrahim, Ishak Ismail, Mohamad Jantan, Yusserie

Zainuddin & Zainal Ariffin Ahmad (Eds.), *Reinventing Asian Management for Global Challenges, Proceedings of The Third Asian Academy of Management Conference*, 333–340.

Arthur, J. B. 1994. Effects of human resource systems on manufacturing performance and turnover. *Academy of Management Journal*, 37: 670–687.

Barney, J. 1991. Firm resources and sustained competitive advantage. *Journal of Management*, 17: 99–120.

Barney, J. B. & Wright, P. M. 1988. On becoming a strategic partner: The role of human resources in gaining competitive advantage. *Human Resource Management*, 37(1): 31–46.

Baird, L. & Meshoulam, I. 1988. Managing the two fits of strategic human resource management. *Academy of Management Review*, 13:116–128.

Boxall, P. & Purcell, J. 2000. Strategic human resource management: Where have we come from and where should we be going? *International Journal of Management Reviews*, 2(2): 183–203.

Chandler, A. D. 1962. *Strategy and Structure: Chapters in the History of American Enterprise*. Boston, MA: MIT Press.

Chang, A. & Huang, T. C. 2005. Relationship between strategic human resource management and firm performance: A contingency perspective. *International Journal of Manpower* 26(5): 434–449.

Cutcher-Gershenfeld, J. 1991. The impact on economic performance of a transformation in workplace relations. *Industrial and Labor Relations Review*, 44:241–260.

Delery, J. E & Doty, D. H. 1996. Modes of theorizing in strategic human resource management: Tests of universalistic, contingency and configurational performance predictions. *Academy of Management Journal*, 39(4): 802–835.

Fombrun, C. J., Tichy, N. M. & Devanna, M. A. 1984. *Strategic Human Resource Management*. London: Wiley.

Gerhart, B. & Milkovich, G. T. 1990. Organizational differences in managerial compensation and financial performance. *Academy of Management Journal*, 33: 663–691.

Golden, K. A. & Ramanujam, V. 1985. Between a dream and a nightmare: On the integration of human resource management and strategic business planning. *Human Resource Management*, 24(4): 429–452.

Greer, C. R. 1995. *Strategy and Human Resources: A General Managerial Perspective*. Englewood Cliffs, NJ: Prentice Hall.

Huselid, M. A. 1995. The impact of human resource management practices on turnover, productivity and corporate financial performance. *Academy of Management Journal*, 38: 635–672.

Huselid, M. A. & Becker, B. E. 1996. Methodological issues in cross-sectional and panel estimates of the human resource-firm performance link. *Industrial Relations*, 35: 400–422.

Huselid, M. A., Jackson, S. E. & Randall, R. S. 1997. Technical and strategic human resource management effectiveness as determinants of firm performance. *Academy of Management Journal*, 40(1): 171–188.

Irwin, J. G., Hoffman, J. J. & Geiger, S. C. 1998. The effects of technological adaptation on organizational performance: Organizational size and environmental munificence as moderators. *The International Journal of Organizational Analysis*, 6(1): 50–64.

Jackson, S. E. & Schuler, R. S. 1995. Understanding human resource management in the context of organizations and their environments. In: M. R. Rosenszweig & L. W. Porter (Eds.), *Annual Review of Psychology*, vol. 46, 237–264.

Kerr, J. L. & Slocum, J. W. 1987. Linking reward systems and corporate cultures. *Academy of Management Executive*, 1(2): 99–108.

Lawler, E. E. III & Mohrman, S. A. 1987. Unions and the new management. *Academy of Management Executive*, 1: 293–300.

Lengnick-Hall, M. L. & Lengnick-Hall, C. A. 1999. Expanding customer orientation in the HR function. *Human Resource Management*, 38(3): 201–214.

Leonard, J. S. 1990. Executive pay and firm performance. *Industrial and Labor Relations Review*, 43: 13–29.

Lundy, O. & Cowling, A. 1996. Organizational culture and motivation in the public sector. the case of the City of Zografou. *Procedia Economics and Finance*, 14: 415–424.

Mabey, C., Salaman, G. & Storey, J. 1998. *Human Resource Management: A Strategic Introduction*. London: Wiley-Blackwell.

MacDuffie, J. P. 1995. Human resource bundles and manufacturing performance: Organizational logic and flexible production systems in the world auto industry. *Industrial and Labor Relations Review*, 48: 197–221.

Majchrzak, A. 1988. *The Human Side of Factory Automation*. San Francisco, CA: Jossey-Bass.

Management Charter Initiative (MCI). 1997. Management standards. Management Charter Initiative (MCI), United Kingdom, April. Available at http://www.bbi.co.uk/whatis.html.

Miles, R. E. & Snow, C. C. 1984. Designing strategic human resources systems. *Organizational Dynamics*, 16: 36–52.

Mintzberg, H. 1987. Crafting strategy. *Harvard Business Review.*

Nee, O. P. & Khatri, N. 1999. Emerging strategic human resource management issues in Singapore. In: Daing Nasir Ibrahim, Ishak Ismail, Mohamad Jantan, Yusserie Zainuddin & Zainal Ariffin Ahmad (Eds.), *Reinventing Asian Management for Global Challenges, Proceedings of the Third Asian Academy of Management Conference*, 311–320.

Ng, I. & Maki, D. 1993. Human resource management in the Canadian manufacturing sector. *The International Journal of Human Resource Management*, 4: 897–916.

Noe, R. A., Hollenbeck, J. R., Gerhart, B. & Wright, P. M. 1997. *Human Resource Management: Gaining a Competitive Advantage*, 2nd Ed. Chicago, IL: Irwin.

Osterman, P. 1987. Choice of employment systems in internal labor markets. *Industrial Relations*, 26: 46–67.

Ouchi, W. G. 1977. The relationship between organizational structure and organizational control. *Administrative Science Quarterly*, 22: 95–113.

Pfeffer, J. 1994. *Competitive Advantage through People: Unleashing the Power of the Workforce*. Boston, MA: Harvard Business School Press.

Porter, M. E. 1980. *Competitive Strategy: Techniques for Analyzing Industries and Competitors*. New York, NY: Free Press (Republished with a new introduction, 1998.)

Porter, M. E. 1985. *The Competitive Advantage: Creating and Sustaining Superior Performance*. New York, NY: Free Press.

Ropo, A. 1993. Towards strategic human resource management: A pilot study in Finnish Power Industry Company. *Personnel Review*, 22(4): 35–53.

Schuler, R. S. 1992. Strategic human resource management: Linking people with the needs of the business. *Organizational Dynamics*, 21(1): 18–32.

Schuler, R. S. & Jackson, S. E. 1987. Linking competitive strategies with human resource management practices. *Academy of Management Executive*, 1: 207–219.

Schuler, R. S. & MacMillan, I. C. 1984. Gaining competitive advantage through human resource practices. *Human Resource Management*, 23: 241–255.

Snell, S. A. & Dean, J. W. 1992. Integrated manufacturing and human resource management: A human capital perspective. *Academy of Management Journal*, 35(3): 467–470.

Sonnenfeld, J. A. & Peiperl, M. A. 1988. Staffing policy as a strategic response: A typology of career systems. *Academy of Management Review*, 13: 588–600.

Takeuchi, N., Wakabayashi, M. & Chen, Z. 2003. The strategic HRM configuration for competitive advantage: Evidence from Japanese firms in China and Taiwan. *Asia Pacific Journal of Management* 20(4): 447–480.

Terpstra, D. E. & Rozell, E. J. 1993. The relationship of staffing practices to organizational level measures of performance. *Personnel Psychology*, 46: 27–48.

Ulrich, D. 1996. *Human Resource Champions*. Boston, MA: Harvard University Press.

Ulrich, D., Brockbank, W., Yeung, A. K. & Lake, D. G. 1995. Human resource competencies: An empirical assessment. *Human Resource Management*, 34(4): 473–495.

Ulrich, D. & Yeung, A. 1989. A shared mindset. *Personnel Administrator*, 117–134.

Wagar, T. H. 1998. Determinants of human resource management practices in small firms: Some evidence from Atlantic Canada. *Journal of Small Business Management*, 36(2): 13–23.

Wright, P. M. & McMahan, G. C. 1992. Theoretical perspectives for strategic human resource management. *Journal of Management*, 18(2): 295–320.

Youndt, M.A., Snell, S.A., Dean, J.W. & Lepak, D.P. 1996. Human resource management, manufacturing strategy, and firm performance. *The Academy of Management Journal*, 39(4): 836–866.

Chapter 2

Strategy: Concept and Process

A study on the creation of the mentioned respected brands and companies reveals their successful alignment of human resource strategies with their business goals, thereby creating organizational capabilities to face an increasingly competitive environment. The developments in the corporate world this reflects prompted me to zero in on my research topic, primarily with the objective of investigating the strategic role of Human Resource Management (HRM) in driving business strategies and goals (Figure 2.1).

A cursory glance at the performance of today's biggest and most formidable global corporation, Walmart, highlights the strategic imperative of the HR function. Sam Walton, who sets the standard for service excellence in the service industry, states that the key to Walmart's success is its positive relationship with its employees.

Information sharing, leadership, employees, motivation, effective use of technology, customer service, quality, innovation and, most importantly, the ability to build a genuine partnership with its employees, or rather, in Walmart's term,

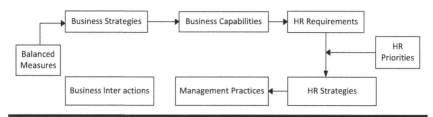

Figure 2.1   A model illustrating how strategic the HR role becomes.

its associates, should be based on the three basic tenets laid down by Walton:

1. Treat employees as partners. Share with them both the good news and the bad so that they will strive to excel and allow them to share in the rewards of their achievement.
2. Encourage employees to always challenge the obvious. The road to success has bearings on both success and failure.
3. Involve associates at all levels in the overall decision-making process, soliciting ideas from all levels of employees.

Strategic HR functions play an important role in viewing and integrating business opportunities, stimulating employees, developing employee strengths and creating corporate teams that share the company's vision and translate that vision into profit.

It has become so significant that every second business leader has one thought: How does one create a global company? It is as if corporate India has suddenly woken up to a world of possibilities overnight. Becoming global will remain the key issue before Indian business leaders for some time now.

The quest for becoming global clearly underscores the importance of HR – building and managing a global organization is a new, hard reality for India Inc. There is a whole range of issues in building a global organization, such as:

1. Managing cultural integration
2. Shaping a new global corporate culture
3. Building a cadre of international managers
4. Developing new capabilities
5. Designing the right organizational structure

In view of the above context, most business leaders in India believe that the key to their success is their people. Their ambitious plans will be constrained by human resources.

As most Indian organizations do not have an in-depth talent pool, unlike Honda, Ford GE etc., they have to design and develop HR systems with a strategic perspective to take on global challenges.

One of the major features of this research study is that it is based on practical research done on MNCs and some big companies to highlight their preparedness toward strategic HRM and also its practices. I have also researched the practices of the world's leading brands like Samsung and GE.

The end result of this research will highlight how we can create a powerful turbo-charged organization with the help of strategic HRM. This research reflects on how strategic HRM practices help these great organizations make the most of their human assets for enduring success.

High-performance companies don't get the extraordinary performers they need by tossing another fad management program on their people; instead, they adhere to fundamental beliefs and operating strategies that pay off in the long run – both in higher profits and more productive employees. The founder and president of the prestigious Saratoga Institute identifies best practices in human asset management in his book *The 8 Practices of Exceptional Companies.*

Based on four years of research involving more than 1,000 companies worldwide and filled with illuminating case studies,

The 8 Practices of Exceptional Companies documents how the best organizations practice:

1. Balanced value fixation
2. Commitment to a core strategy
3. Culture-system linkage
4. Massive two-way communication
5. Partnering with stakeholders
6. Functional collaboration
7. Innovation and risk
8. Never being satisfied

It is clear from the research that managers and executives need to shift their primary focus away from short-term process improvements (reengineering, benchmarking and quality) and toward enduring human asset management practices that can make these efforts long-term successes.

It Is Imperative for the Corporate World to Design Strategic HR Management

In today's intensely competitive and unforgiving marketplace, maintaining a competitive advantage by becoming a low-cost leader or a differentiator puts a heavy premium on having a highly engaged workforce with excellent competence levels. A sustainable competitive advantage lies not just in differentiating a product or service or in becoming a low-cost leader but in being able to tap the company's portfolio of skills in order to respond to the customer's needs and the competitor's moves.

In a growing number of organizations, human resources are now viewed as a source of competitive advantage. There is greater recognition that distinctive competencies are obtained through highly developed employee skills, distinctive organizational cultures, management processes and systems. This is in contrast to the traditional emphasis on transferable resources such as equipment. It is being increasingly recognized that a sustainable competitive advantage can be obtained with a high-quality workforce that enables organizations to compete on the basis of market responsiveness, product and service quality, differentiated products and technological innovation.

Strategic Human Resource Management has been defined as the linking of human resources with strategic goals and objectives in order to improve business performance and develop an organizational culture that fosters innovation and flexibility. Strategic HR means accepting the HR function as a strategic partner in the formulation of the company's strategies as well as in the implementation of those strategies through activities such as recruiting, selecting, training and rewarding personnel. While strategic HR recognizes HR's partnership role in the strategizing process, the term HR strategies refers to specific HR courses of action the company plans to pursue in order to achieve its aims. HR management can play an important role in environment scanning, i.e., identifying and analyzing external opportunities and threats that may be crucial to the company's success. Similarly, HR management also provides Competitive Intelligence that may be useful in driving strategic planning processes.

While designing strategic Human Resource Management policies, one needs to ask these three key questions:

1. What are the internal and external variables that impact on the ability of the organization to devise and deliver a strategic approach to managing people?
2. How does human resource strategy influence everyday human behavior?
3. What impact do human resource interventions have on the individuals?

Strategic HRM ensures that people processes are a source of competitive advantage. The key challenge that organizations faced in the late 1990s was to deliver a sustained competitive advantage in the short term while at the same time preparing for longer-term success. Although the principal source of competitive advantage in the past decade may have been access to financial resources or usage of the latest technology, these are now viewed as necessary but not sufficient.

For most progressive companies the sources of competitive advantage lie not only in access to finance, capital or technology but within the organization, in people and processes capable of delivering customer satisfaction and rapid innovation, which will keep them ahead of competitors.

Process Improvements to Move toward Enduring Human Resource Management

Strategic HRM Helps to Create Employer Branding

In 2001 a study was conducted which found that many large organizations were using the methodology of a corporate brand building strategy to attract and keep quality employees. The study found that employer branding was being used by 40% of respondents in a survey of 138 leading companies to increase their attractiveness to potential and current employees. Yet most of the initiatives were relatively new, and many started in the year 2000. However, funding and awareness of "Employer Branding" seems to be increasing, particularly in companies whose corporate brand image is not strong among the general public because they are operating in the B2B segment and not in the B2C segment. In other words, prospective employees are not likely to have heard of them.

Role of Strategic HRM for Achieving Global Ambitions

Becoming a powerful global player is an imperative, not a choice, for the world's largest companies – and those that aspire to join their ranks.

Research has shown that the best global companies – the global champions, the top 60 companies in the world – clearly outperform market indices over long periods of time and handle global volatility very well.

In such companies, HRM plays a very strategic role toward preparing the companies for global dominance.

Research shows that becoming global requires three critical steps:

1. Developing a winning formula of distinctive capabilities that is used to secure the home base but can also be easily transferred across multiple geographies.
2. Grooming a cadre of global executives who can customize the formula into these new geographies.
3. Mastering an international organizational matrix of businesses, geographies and functions so that these well-apprenticed executives can operate effectively.

Building capabilities, executives and an organization that can operate across national boundaries is far more important than deciding which markets to enter and when. In fact, there is a vast difference between "going global" and "becoming global." Simply stated, becoming global is about adopting a global approach and mindset across the business model. It is a long journey fraught with peril, in which managers must constantly ask the following question:

"Do our actions help build a company that can beat the best in the world?" Only a few will truly be able to answer "Yes".

Embarking on a Journey

Successful globalization results from systematically overcoming traditional disadvantages through the three primary activities mentioned above:

Working Out a Winning Formula

The competitive advantage in any market accrues through distinctive capabilities, privileged local relationships or valuable assets or rights (for example, mining concessions) that a company possesses. Companies that rely solely on local privileged relationships or valuable assets or rights for the competitive advantage remain trapped in an export mentality and rarely become one of the top global companies in their industry. Research clearly demonstrates that global leaders are those that have developed a set of world-class capabilities into a winning formula that can be put into practice globally.

A battle-tested winning formula will help a company generate above-normal profits in most of the markets it enters. This has indeed been the case of CEMEX; the Mexican cement giant realized that it could manage its plants more efficiently by using advanced production technology to lower production costs along with efficient distribution networks to deliver orders speedily. By the early 1990s, the Mexican plants owned by CEMEX were the most efficient in the United States, using satellite technology to monitor production performance and dispatch orders quickly.

Grooming a Global Cadre of Executives

Successfully transferring the winning formula into new markets requires a group of global executives who are well-versed in both the company's operating practices and the new country's business culture.

Research shows that a methodical approach to building a cadre of global executives is much more important to global companies than tangible plant, property or equipment.

For global companies, it is always preferred that executives are groomed from within, beginning with locally recruited entry-level executives. Such executives can be fully trained in a company's processes and operating methods while retaining the ability to customize these practices to their own culture.

A major IT company based in India has begun recruiting from top-tier US business schools with the specific objective of grooming globally mobile executives. It has created two separate career tracks, one for the domestic market and one for international markets, with distinct recruitment, job rotation and compensation policies. These efforts are paying off as this new crop of global executives, able to combine relationship management skills and offshore development knowledge, begins to sell high-end solutions to large accounts.

Global job rotation is crucial to grooming global executives. Such practices typically target the creation of an expert general manager, someone with deep functional expertise in a single area and also a CEO-type cross-functional perspective with high cultural sensitivity.

HSBC, for example, puts 400 handpicked "international managers" through a global rotation program to expose them to various situations, training them to parachute into troubled operations and fix those problems.

CEMEX's program assigns top-performing executives to M&A, due diligence and post-merger management projects in foreign countries where they are also trained to understand different cultures.

Mastering the International Matrix

The cadre of global executives makes a global organization more feasible. Coordination processes run smoothly because they trust each other. A dotted-line reporting relationship works because executives know each other well. Much business gets done informally through social contacts. Job rotations provide a well-rounded perspective on challenges in other markets. Entrenched power structures are avoided, and institutions become stronger than any group of individuals.

Creating a cohesive company culture that transcends national boundaries is a crucial aspect of becoming global.

The best global companies have a distinct way of doing business and have developed a set of specific, unifying values and informal networks.

As companies begin competing in markets around the world, they need to adapt their organizational structure into a three-dimensional matrix of businesses, geographies and functions. Such a set-up for allocating activities and decision rights is crucial to ensuring operational control and capturing global-scale economies while enabling local management to retain some flexibility. Some decisions like marketing, production mix and pricing are best left to local units, while others like brand values, financing and overall strategy are best kept centralized.

A company that is globalizing its operations chooses from three common organizational models:

1. End-to-end global business units
2. End-to-end geographic units
3. Hybrid model where some functions (for example, manufacturing and R&D) remain centralized while others like sales, servicing and marketing are geographically dispersed.

The end-to-end global business unit model works well when businesses are quite distinct, do not share any common operations and sell to different customers.

The end-to-end geographic unit works well when a business requires a localized value chain and caters to local customers. Businesses that tend to be local (for example, restaurants, cement and financial services) typically follow this approach.

Since the global journey is lengthy, and most local leaders will not be able to keep up the pace, they have to concentrate on the following critical issues having HR and other strategic dimensions:

CRITICAL ISSUES (BUSINESS AND OPERATION PERSPECTIVE)

1. Does the management have the ambition and determination to be a global player?
2. Does the entire team share the ambition?
3. Are they mentally prepared for the long journey (5–15 years on average)?
4. Can the home market position generate adequate cash flows to support an expensive and often error-prone globalization effort?
5. Has the company achieved operational excellence in basic business operations so that processes are reliable and operating at world-class levels?
6. Which distinctive capabilities will allow the company to make money outside the home markets?
7. How should new capabilities be built to open new markets?

CRITICAL ISSUES (PEOPLE AND ORGANIZATION PERSPECTIVE)

1. Who is going to lead the charge in the overseas market?
2. Does the company have enough home-grown leaders to operate effectively in these new markets?
3. How many people need to be hired and how will they be inducted into hard core business?
4. At a broader level, how should the organizational structure and management process be changed to integrate into an international business?
5. How will the socialization process be designed for the people working in international operations so that they feel connected to the company and its culture?

The globalization challenges are worth taking on as the potential rewards are plentiful. Global leaders are likely to achieve the size, competitiveness and broad market presence to succeed and endure in increasingly turbulent global markets.

Strategic HRM plays an increasingly important role by helping the ambitious company to win the war for talent. The war for talent is real, and it is keeping Indian CEOs awake at night. The reason is simple: Indian firms never had a cadre of managers trained to operate in international markets. As many of the companies in the BW Global 100 begin expanding across international markets, scarcity of senior managers who can lead the charge is forcing the company heads to slow the pace of growth.

Lateral hiring at senior levels is the obvious solution, and an increasing number of Indian companies are doing the same.

As regards industry practices, the cases of Asian Paints, L&T, Berger etc. drive home the above point.

The following Case-lets highlight the globalization drive of a few top Indian companies.

CASE-LET OF TATA MOTORS

Tata Motors has begun to erase the word "exports" from its lexicon. The new motto inside India's largest automaker is "international," and it is already rolling out a series of initiatives to make that transition. For starters, exports will now be just one part of the international business. Then, not just the new line of trucks, even sourcing of parts will become global; Tata managers will hunt out parts, wherever they are available at the lowest cost, especially for all new vehicles.

The most interesting changes are in the product development process. Earlier, the domestic market team led the process; now, people across the globe study international markets and then put their insights together to make the basic product. Now, the sales teams are made to sit together in monthly steering committee meetings. This is to force people to think differently. Now, a person could be discussing opportunities in Kerala, Jammu and Kashmir and Southeast Asia for the same platform.

Ravi Kant, executive director of Tata Motors, says: "It is important to break all the barriers and make the organization a boundary-less one. Now, the international team is no longer detached from the domestic business. They have to compare costs, and targets are set against benchmarks.

It is only a mindset change."

CASE-LET OF NIIT

Consider the case of NIIT, which tried "exporting" its culture abroad in the initial phases of its globalization journey. In the early days, the company even replicated its Indian HR manual in its international offices. That created an interesting situation. For instance, casual leave was mandatory in India but unheard of in the United States; however, NIIT offered it anyway. Since then, the company has progressively decentralized. "We initially saw ourselves as a global company with a local presence," says Vijay Thadani, CEO of NIIT. But now each outpost sees itself as a local company with a parent – one that happens to be present in 32 other countries.

Thadani cites the example of his office in the United States. The company had hired a new team consisting of a COO and 15 Americans, pushing up the total strength from 35 to 50. "As soon as the team walked in and tasted the coffee, they simply hated it and immediately ordered a gourmet coffee counter from Starbucks," says Thadani. This created a few ripples among the Indian staff. They were used to working with a tight budget. And now it seemed that the budgets had been hiked for the newcomers. Indian management did not think that the coffee machine was needed, it would not interfere. That they were free to run the company the way they wanted... and that NIIT believed its growth was the derivative of its employees' growth," adds Thadani.

So what is the glue that holds the entire organization together? For NIIT and many others, it is a somewhat amorphous thing called values. Thadani says that at the lower level are all the local nuances – holidays, HR manuals, compensation and so on; at a higher level is the value system. "And this stays the same for all companies. Values are the same across all human beings. They don't change," he says.

CASE-LET OF INDIAN HOTELS

Many Indian firms are coaching their executives on appropriate business etiquette in foreign lands, preparing country dossiers and conducting sensitivity workshops. But no amount of training quite prepares them for cross-cultural challenges. Experience is the best tutor.

Like it was for Christine F. Jamal, vice-president at Indian Hotels, back in the late 1980s. Indian Hotels had just acquired St James' Court in London, and Jamal was dispatched with a team from the head office in Mumbai to manage it. The hotel wasn't fully staffed; all senior managers were expected to roll up their sleeves and jump into customer service with alacrity.

Jamal and her team got a rude shock. Indians are naturally hospitable; they would go out of their way to make guests feel comfortable. Jamal soon realized international travelers didn't really like the invasion of their privacy. Once she walked up to two gentlemen standing near the counter and asked if she could be of any help. The guests looked startled and said they didn't need any. Jamal overheard them saying no one had ever asked them this before.

Jamal thought she had learned a valuable lesson, only to be proved wrong a few days later. A foreign tourist had been slightly injured and began to raise a huge fuss about not getting medical attention. It took Jamal enormous effort to convince her that no stone would be left unturned to attend to her medical needs. Lesson number two: for most part, foreigners like being left alone, but on certain occasions, they demand special attention.

One day, Jamal received a job application from a local. He was a good candidate, except that there was a gap in his career. The man had taken time off to travel to China and the Far East for over six months. Jamal was about to discard the application, putting it down as a perceived lack of focus, when a colleague intervened: "Such people are great value additions for a hotel because of the wealth of cross-cultural experience they bring." The hunch was right – and changed the hotel's hiring strategy forever.

CASE STUDY OF BHARAT FORGE

The issues aren't only about the people within. As Indian companies use overseas M&A as a route to globalize, equally important will be managing the people of the acquired firm. This is currently Baba Kalyani's biggest challenge. The Bharat Forge chairman snapped up CDC, a German forgings company. Now, to make this acquisition work, much depends on his integration program. If Kalyani and his senior managers from India can retain the talent and make their German counterparts believe that an Indian company can look after their interests, Bharat Forge may be able to leverage the high-end engineering skills that the Germans are best known for and thus move up the auto component value chain. It's no surprise that Kalyani now spends a number of days each month in Germany working with the local German managers.

Cultural integration can be a tricky issue. A few years back, to move up the value chain, Infosys Technologies was close to buying Cambridge Technology Partners. The deal fell through for many reasons. One key reason was that Infosys Technologies wasn't sure whether it would be able to retain Cambridge's consultants after the buyout.

Inside corporate India's boardrooms, it is now acknowledged that people can make the difference between successfully globalizing or not. In the context of the difference between his company and competitor Honda, TVS Motor CEO Venu Srinivasan puts it succinctly. "Ultimately, all our growth plans will be constrained by human resources. Our human resources pool is very small compared to (that of) Honda. No Indian company has a ready human resource pool," he says.

Some would argue that Indian CEOs, especially those in manufacturing, are simply unwilling to pay more for talent. McKinsey principal Ramesh Mangaleswaran observes that unless CEOs change the way they are willing to reward top-flight talent, this mindset could well become a blocker". He says the problem can become especially acute for Indian companies that need to build market access in Europe or the United States.

Bibliography

Alchian, A. A. & Demsetz, H. 1972. Production, information costs, and economic organization. *American Economic Review*, 62(December): 777–795.

Armstrong, M. 2006. *A Handbook of Human Resource Management Practice*, 10th Ed. Cambridge University Press.

Armstrong, M. 2006. *Performance Management: Key Strategies and Practical Guidelines*, 3rd Ed. London: Kogan Page Limited

Armstrong, M. 2006. *Strategic Human Resource Management: A Guide to Action*, 3rd Ed. Dexter, MI: Thomson-Shore, Inc.

Boxall, P. & Purcell, J. 2003. *Strategy and Human Resource Management*. Basingstoke and New York: Palgrave Macmillan.

Boxall, P., Purcell, J. & Wright, P. 2007. The Oxford handbook of "Human resource management". In: B. Gerhart (Ed.), *Modeling HRM and Performance Linkages*, 552–580. Cape Town: Oxford University Press.

Boxall, P., Purcell, J. & Wright, P. 2007. The Oxford handbook of Human resource management. In: G. Latham, L. M. Sulsky & H. MacDonald (Eds.), *Performance Management*, 364–384. Cape Town: Oxford University press.

Boxall, P., Purcell, J. & Wright, P. 2007. The Oxford handbook of Human resource management. In: J. Purcell & N. Kinnie (Eds.), *HRM and Business Performance*, 533–551. Cape Town: Oxford University press.

Brewster, C. et al. 2000. *Contemporary Issues in Human Resource Management: Gaining a Competitive Advantage*. Cape Town: Oxford University Press.

Brumbach, G. B. 1 Dec 1988. Some ideas, issues and predictions about performance management. *Public Personnel Management*, 17(4), Winter: 387–402.

Campbell, J. P. 1999. The definition and measurement of performance in the new age. In: D. R. Ilgen & E. D. Pulakos (Eds.), *The Changing Nature of Performance: Implications for Staffing, Motivation, and Development*, 399–429. San Francisco, CA: Jossey-Bass.

Dyer, L. & Reeves, T., 1995. *Human Resource Strategies and Firm Performance: What Do We Know and Where Do We Need to Go?* Paper presented at the 10th World Congress of the International Industrial Relations Association, Washington, DC.

Guest, D. E. 1987. Human resource management and industrial relations. *Journal of Management Studies,* 24(5): 503–521.

Guest, D. E. 2011. Human resource management and performance: Still searching for some answers. *Human Resource Management Journal,* 21(1): 3–13.

Hendry, C. & Pettigrew, A. 1990. Human resource management: An agenda for the 1990s. *International Journal of Human Resource Management,* 1: 17–43.

Holbeche, L. 8 June 2004. How to make work more meaningful. *Personnel Today,* 26.

Janssens, M. & Steyaert, C. 2009. HRM and performance: A plea for reflexivity in HRM studies. *Journal of Management Studies,* 46(1): 143–155.

Lance, C. E. 1994. Test of a latent structure of performance ratings derived from Wherry's (1952) theory of ratings. *Journal of Management,* 20: 757–771.

Lifson, K. A. 1953. Errors in time-study judgments of industrial work pace. *Psychological Monographs,* 67(355).

Noe, R., Hollenbeck, J. R., Gerhart, B. & Wright, P. M. 2007. *Fundamentals of Human Resource Management,* 2nd Ed. Boston, MA: McGraw-Hill.

Venkatraman, N. & Ramanujam, V. 1986. Measurement of business performance in strategy research: A comparison of approaches. *Academy of Management Review,* 11: 801–814.

Chapter 3

Strategic Human Resource Management: Concept and Process

Competitive Human Resources Strategies

Today's business growth strategies provide a window of opportunity to shape a more meaningful HR agenda, and a practical but thoughtful approach for tying the HR strategy to the growth plans of the company should be pursued jointly by corporate HR teams and their divisional counterparts, with the close involvement of line leaders. A 4-step process for creating a strategic HR agenda is outlined, and the experiences of various companies are compared.

Innovations in business strategy, especially in the race to find new sources of growth, have created new pressures to refocus human resources work, roles and priorities. In smaller, entrepreneurial firms, the CEO/founder fights a war to attract, retain and motivate bright, young and technically able people. In large, multi-national companies, the impact of people on the competitiveness of businesses has become increasingly clear, and HR professionals are being asked to help create strategic clarity across the organization.

Human resources strategy has evolved through various forms over the past 20 years. Respected companies like IBM, Digital Equipment and Merck & Co. pioneered the early efforts to create HR strategies, which aimed to tie human resources functional strategies to business priorities. Flynt-Vega (1998) identified a positive relationship between the shareholder value and the extent of strategic HR work performed in the 740 firms studied. Ulrich (1997) has written at length about the need to redefine HR roles into strategic partnerships that provide more value to external customers. Brockbank (1999) has presented a 4-stage lifecycle model for characterizing the extent to which the HR function is strategic, arguing that firms should move from being reactive and finally, in a few cases to becoming strategically proactive.

Today another transition is underway, as companies like Warner-Lambert, Coca-Cola, Colgate-Palmolive, Whirlpool and others are actively seeking new ways to define pragmatic, but innovative, people strategies that will directly support the business agendas that drive stock prices and expectations for growing the shareholder value.

The key is to focus resources – to select a growth highway – rather than spreading resources across many options. Focusing on the growth highway is the means to making hard choices:

- All companies seek growth through some mix of market share gains within current and new segments, geographies, acquisitions, etc.
- Most companies that return long-term value growth for shareholders are unusual in that they focus on one primary growth path – or maybe two.

Implications for Human Resources Strategy

Ulrich (1998) has argued that a business demonstrates the capability of "strategic clarity" when its strategy focuses on both short-term and long-term goals, creates meaning for those inside and outside the company, translates vision into effective organizational practices, shapes employee behaviors and differentiates the firm to customers and investors.

The search for strategic business focus demands greater clarity of HR focus. HR practices play a key role in creating close alignment of behavior to the selected growth highway. The top leadership at Whirlpool, for example, has made it clear that their growth path depends on a culture of great focus on consumer-focused brand building and on global processes for product creation. The company has launched major efforts to create and reward innovation in its culture and brand building tool kit. The implications for "people plans" are numerous.

What Does an Effective HR Agenda Need to Do?

Today's business challenges demand a focused human resources agenda. To close the gap between the "strategic-HR haves" and "have-nots," practitioners need a thoughtful, but practical, approach to accomplishing the following:

- Force a set of clear choices – connect the people priorities to business priorities.
- Clarify line ownership for HR outcomes and reach a contract for the responsibility HR people will have.
- Guide the allocation of people investments to the most important activities.

- Drive energy upstream – toward the things that produce more impact.
- Define the organizational and systems framework for the HR function across its business units.
- Energize people with a sense of purpose.

Why Do So Few HR Strategies Provide These Benefits?

In order to avoid the gaps between strategy and execution that Ulrich and Lake (1990) and others have described, today's approaches to HR strategy should avoid past mistakes. Among the problems to be avoided are:

- Too much complexity
- Lack of depth of thinking in the end product
- Over-focus on "best practices" and fads rather than strategy choices
- Lack of line-leader involvement and the belief that HR strategies are for HR people
- Murky definition of strategy roles and expectations among enterprise vs. business units
- Lack of capabilities within the HR organization to execute their responsibility for the plans

These challenges can be overcome by paying attention to 4 tasks.

Four Steps to an HR Agenda

The challenge in the strategy process is to deliver depth of thinking without complexity and to do it in a manner that involves line people in the process. Our experience with more than 20 large companies points to 4 elements or tasks that need to be accomplished, roughly in the following sequence, to produce a meaningful HR strategy in large, divisionalized companies:

- Enterprise People Philosophies and Themes – View from the top (CEO and SVP/HR).
- Business Unit People Plans – Tied directly to the business unit strategies.
- Company-Wide HR Priorities – Set of common priorities, practices and policies across the enterprise.
- HR Operations Plans – Action-oriented plans to build the effectiveness of the HR organization, with a 2–3-year time frame.

Step 1: Enterprise People Philosophies and Themes

Human resources work becomes a priority for line management when the chief executive and his/her chief HR officer demonstrate a strong point of view about the role people play in the business.

The CEO and the chief human resources officer should provide an umbrella for defining all HR priorities, a view from the top that defines the role of people in making the enterprise competitive: overarching themes related to vision, values and corporate strategy. These themes are often identified by teams chartered by the CEO or the chief HR officer. In other cases, they reflect primarily the personal beliefs of the top leaders. These priorities have the most traction when a challenge or goal is set out for senior operating managers who create pressure for business unit leaders to define their own people plans that address the challenges that the CEO and top HR officer have laid out.

The new CEO at a large pharmaceutical company, supported by the senior vice president of human resources, chartered a team of high-potential employees to complete a study and implement a set of recommendations under the heading of Workforce 2000.

In dialogue with leaders across the corporation, the action-learning team defined 4 "business builders": process focus, alliance capability, IT uptake and knowledge management. They then defined a set of "organizational enablers," which became the center of the new chairman's expectations with general managers: leadership depth, talent management, education, teaming capabilities and diverse people and structures. This umbrella became the anchor for defining people priorities in the business.

Sears, Roebuck and Co. provides a more specific example of a challenging, high-level people agenda, owned directly by its chairman, Arthur Martinez and its former, top HR officer, Anthony Rucci. Together, Martinez and Rucci deployed the "employee-customer-profit chain," a model that demonstrated a statistical link between employee motivation and shopper loyalty. The profit chain demanded that leaders throughout the organization focus energies on making Sears a compelling place to work, a compelling place to shop and a compelling place to invest. While Sears' challenges remain difficult, a successful turnaround was launched in the mid-1990s, and the employee-customer profit chain was a key element of focusing those energies. Whirlpool has adopted a similar approach; each business unit leader defines their own version of a people plan, but they must have a plan and it must support the larger organizational agenda for growth. At both Sears and Whirlpool, the strength in the people agenda is in the high degree of participation in learning that took place in each of the organizations.

Potential Action Items

- Build a "story" based on the personal beliefs of the CEO and the top HR officer with regard to people and organization.
- Help the CEO to set a challenge to line leaders with a few key themes that place people high on corporate priorities.
- Adopt a standard and a message for business units to follow.
- Focus the HR policy committee on an overall planning process and launch an inclusive planning process.

Step 2: Business Unit People Plan

A business unit people plan is the second piece of the overall HR agenda. Each business unit develops its own plan. These would be built into the strategic and operating plans of the business units and major functions – completed jointly by HR and line executives. It represents people planning at the front lines of business. These line-of-business people plans are to HR planning what "competitive strategy" is to business planning. They address people and organizational issues that are directly related to serving customers, winning against competitors, and growing the revenue and profits of the business unit. Unit people plans should:

- Help focus line leaders on strategic HR work.
- Help focus HR people on business priorities.
- Define mutual expectations for the roles of line and HR people.
- Define measures.
- Identify issues that need to be directed to corporate "centers-of-expertise" to ensure the alignment of programs and initiatives.

The link between business plans and people plans begins with defining the key organizational capabilities.

Organizational Capabilities – Path to People Plans

Dave Ulrich (1998) has described capabilities as the missing link between strategy and action. Organizations, as distinct from the people who run them, demonstrate capabilities if the capabilities meet the following criteria:

- Offer integration: Capabilities are not a matter of individual competence or management systems but are organizationally based.
- Add value to customers: Defined by those outside the firm as important.
- Offer uniqueness: They cannot easily be copied by competitors.
- Engage employee commitment: Capabilities create meaning for employees.
- Maintain continuity: Capabilities remain relatively stable over time.

The role of HR is largely aimed at translating growth strategies into growth capabilities. Capabilities are the result of HR work. So capabilities are the most logical bridge between the business growth plan and the HR priorities over a 2- or 3-year period of time. Once a set of capabilities is defined, HR results can be identified by asking, "Which levers will create those capabilities?" Kessler and McClellan (1996) defined the relationship between capabilities, business growth opportunities and the 3 levers that are likely to produce the most impact on capabilities:

1. Individual competencies
2. Business processes and structure
3. Culture and behavior

Organization Capabilities Defining the Work of HR in Supporting the Growth Strategy of the Business

The Competency Lever

The role of individual competencies in building organizational capabilities seems intuitive, and yet most companies that invest large amounts of time and resources in developing competency models (another HR fad) have spent precious little time linking them to organizational-capability requirements. Coca-Cola, on the other hand, has focused senior executive energy on identifying human capital plans for all business units, as well as the enterprise, with great emphasis on defining both the capability (know-how mix) and the capacity (staffing levels) requirements to execute their worldwide growth strategies (Figure 3.1).

A large sector of a Fortune 50 services company defined a set of 7 capabilities critical to achieving its growth plans. The capabilities were then translated into individual leadership and functional competencies (Table 3.1). The selected business growth path required depth in positioning and branding, as well as more effective management of key constituencies.

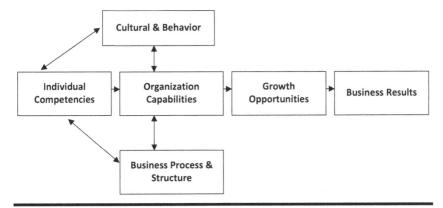

Figure 3.1   Organization capabilities defining the work of HR in supporting the growth strategy of the business.

Table 3.1   Capabilities and Individual Competencies at a Sector of a Fortune 50 Service Company

Organizational Capabilities		Individual Competencies That Support Them
• Stakeholder Focus and Understanding • Product and Service Management • Flexibility • Business Transformation • Information Systems & Operational Execution • Relationship Management • Branding and Positioning	→	• Product Knowledge • Branding and Positioning • Pricing • Continuous Quality Improvement • Financial Skills • Project Management • Leadership Dimensions

Table 3.2   Business Priorities and Organizational Capabilities

Business Priorities	Organizational Capabilities	People Priorities
• Drivers for Growth • Critical Objectives • Key Business Initiatives	• Business Process & structure Improvements • Individual Competencies • Culture/Behavior Needs	• Key HR Outputs & measures • Key HR Projects, Interventions, Tools • Key Linkages
To Win in Our Markets	*Requirements vs. Current = Gaps*	*Actions to Close Gaps*

An assessment process was then launched to measure the current depth of its competencies. A set of talent strategies was developed for each major department, aimed at elevating the overall presence of the requisite competencies (Table 3.2).

The Process and Structure Lever

Process and organization structure are the second lever in the divisional people plan. Stalk et al. (1992) defined the role that a business process plays in building capabilities, arguing as many others have, that the key is building process capabilities that cross functions. HR leaders are in a unique position to act as influencers for building these process capabilities. A large consumer durables company, we shall call "ABC Co.," has invested great energies in deploying its global product-development process. HR leaders at ABC have played a significant role in execution. Executives wisely discovered that global product-development required organizational fixes: breaking down boundaries, growing a deeper bench of project leaders, rewarding innovation, deploying technology talent more effectively and making global teams effective. The HR strategy for ABC's global product-development organization was exclusively focused on these kinds of issues.

The Culture Lever

Culture is the third lever in the people plan. Its impact on capability is well documented. Culture and behavior may be the toughest change-management challenge in executing the growth strategy. Proctor and Gamble's recent efforts to reinvent itself amounts to a full assault on the "P&G way." The new CEO, Dirk Jager, is convinced that P&G's historically celebrated culture traits and splintered organization structure are now obstacles to innovation, risk-taking and speed, demonstrated in repeated failures to beat Colgate-Palmolive and others in new, global product introductions.

The role of HR in driving these kinds of changes varies widely among companies, but if the HR community has not defined priorities in this arena it is not in the game.

Involving Line Leaders in the Capabilities Discussion

The participation of line leadership in building the divisional people plan is critical. When it works best, HR leaders are asking hard questions for line people to answer and those answers are built into the business strategy.

The objective of HR leaders should be to push for deeper levels of thinking and content through these kinds of questions:

■ What is the key growth path in our business strategy?
■ What are the critical organizational capabilities required to exploit those opportunities?
■ What business processes and organizational designs must be created to create those capabilities?
■ What are the individual competencies (skills, knowledge and attributes) that people must have to be successful?
■ How does the culture need to reinforce behavior to achieve the capabilities?
■ What are our current gaps in this regard?
■ How will we close those gaps?

It is helpful to have a planning template that will guide the dialogue in major divisions or business units. The template should be common-sense oriented. Coca-Cola, USA, uses a template (tailored by other companies) that clarifies the relationship between business priorities, organizational capabilities and its people priorities for the operating unit.

Each of the cells in the models is "filled in" by preparing drafts and then reviewing them with line leaders to gain consensus. Numerous tools are available to help with that work, and the process provides an action-learning challenge for HR people in the business units, who often work together to complete the content.

The sequence of events in the planning process in this company flowed as follows:

■ Workshop 1: Division and location HR people learn the corporate people priorities and review division strategy themes, as well as a set of diagnostic tools, for returning to their organizations to conduct capabilities interviews.

- Interviews were completed and raw data summarized.
- Workshop 2: Participants learn analysis methods and work in teams to analyze the capabilities data. Scenarios are prepared.
- Scenarios are reviewed with line leaders back in the units.
- Plans are drafted by intact HR teams, based on all inputs.

Step 3: Company-Wide People Priorities

The objective of this step of the strategy process is to define the degree of integration or commonality that is needed among HR practices – across the various business units – to move the business forward. "What are the ties that bind?" asked one HR officer during the planning process? Defining the right degree of common ability in HR policy, practice and objectives among units is a challenging but healthy dialogue, which needs to be crafted, not left to chance or political wrangling. When it is not resolved in a deliberate fashion, corporate and divisional or sector HR leaders struggle with autonomy questions as frustrated line partners look on.

A powerful, common-sense solution is reached when the leaders of the various HR units work together to answer these three questions:

- What are the "top 10" people objectives for the entire company which we share?
- Which policies and practices are core, and which should be designed to be business unit specific?
- What initiatives will HR units manage together over the next 3 years as well as the next 12 months (in order to deliver the top 10 objectives)?

These decisions offer more than a consolidation of the business unit or department people plans. They provide an integrated view of the people strategy. Today's business growth highways require a clear picture of how integrated the businesses and their people practices need to be. Examples are plentiful: product development cannot be effectively managed in divisionalized silos; brands cannot be leveraged around the world with regional decisions about positioning and advertising messages; global customers, like power-retail trade partners and others, cannot be managed without highly coordinated global teams and systems. In each of these examples, HR practices should influence those outcomes. Without a big-picture view of people priorities, this is not likely.

Today's HR information system (HRIS) strategies create obvious pressure to resolve integration requirements across the corporation. Legitimate differences in HR practices exist between businesses within the same enterprise when one business unit markets benefit-management services to large healthcare providers and another develops pharmaceutical products. But the systems support requirements should reflect the areas of necessary linkage between the two or risk wasteful and ineffective systems support.

References

Brockbank, W. 1999. If HR were really strategically proactive: Present and future directions in HR's contribution to competitive advantage. *Human Resource Management*, 38(4): 337–352.

Flynt-Vega, T. 1997. *Hustled: My Journey from Fear to Faith.* Westminster: John Knox Press.

Kessler & McClellan. 1996. *Liability v. Innovation.* https://liabilityinnovation.files.wordpress.com/2015/11/kessler-mcclellan-1996.pdf

Stalk, G., Evans, P. & Shulman, L. 1992. Competing on capabilities: The new rules of corporate strategy. *Harvard Business Review*, 70, 57–69.

Ulrich, D. 1997: HR of the future: Conclusions and observations. *Human Resource Management*, 38(1): 175–179.

Ulrich, D. 1998. A new mandate for human resources *Harvard Business Review*, January–February 1998.

Chapter 4

Formulating and Implementing HR Strategies

Corporate Governance and the HR Agenda

At the two extremes of the corporate–governance continuum (holding-company models vs. one-product companies), it is relatively clear how much commonality should be incorporated into the HR agenda. In general, HR governance should reflect the corporate governance model. HR functions that struggle most with confusion over roles between corporate staff and divisional or regional HR staff (and many companies still do struggle with these issues) are those in which the enterprise operates with mixed governance models. Many companies move the pendulum back and forth between very loose and very tight control over profit centers, while others simply evolve toward one or the other. In our experience, HR leadership can help draw attention to these issues, and can actually help force the dialogue and create more clarity with regard to overall corporate governance.

Global Integration

Defining the extent of global integration among practice areas is part of decision-making in "Step 3" of the strategy model. And it is here that the decisions often include a mix of company-wide vs. unit-specific differences, driven by local-national or regional differences that are very difficult to bridge. The executive-talent pool practices at IBM, Colgate-Palmolive and others are highly communized and supported by integrated systems. But in those same companies, regional and local-national differences in compensation practice remain (due to regulatory and culture barriers), while common principles are utilized. It is important to be deliberate when selecting the degrees of "sameness and of difference."

Most Commonly Integrated Global Practices

Our study of global companies indicated the most commonly integrated practices across all geographies are:

■ Worldwide leadership competency models – "global vocabulary" for talent.
■ Key executive data system – top 2–5% of managers.
■ General management talent pool program for "global high-potential leaders." Increased recruiting of "global leaders" – third-country nationals.
■ Action-learning as a business-strategy process and a means to implement change.

The logic of the discussion should flow something like this:

1. What practices are most critical to support corporate integration? (Which practices need to be "common" across the company and around the world?)

2. What degree of commonality is needed, for each practice area, and how should it be achieved?
3. From where (and by whom) should each of the practices be managed?

Adapting the ideas of Schuler et al. (1991) the author has helped company-wide HR councils, led by a senior HR officer, to identify degrees of necessary integration and to pinpoint the needs for various practice areas on a five-point scale (see Table 4.1). This model refers to the difference between the common HR philosophies and the strategic decisions being taken. Common tools are only likely to provide integration when there is a communized view of the philosophy, strategy and policy.

In companies like Coca-Cola, Merck, Praxair and many others, a single competency model provides the integration of talent initiatives, while differences in regional or divisional practices are allowed or encouraged based on the specific nature of the talent gaps (Table 4.1).

Table 4.1   Finding Core vs. Business-Specific Practices

	Common Principles and Philosophies	*Common Policies or Practices*	*Common Tools and Controls*
Performance management			
Base and incentive pay			
Strategic staffing (assess, select and develop)			
Management learning and education			

Potential Action Items

Interview top executives in the company regarding high-level priorities.

1. Understand what the corporate governance model means for HR.
2. Consolidate key business-unit capability gaps – direct those issues into corporate centers-of-expertise.
3. Dialogue and debate within the HR policy committee – build alignment and consensus.
4. Take drafts back to line leaders for more dialogue.
5. Determine who will need to work together in the HR community for the next 18–24 months to meet expectations.

Step 4: HR-Organization Renewal (Operational Plans)

Many companies completed multiple iterations of HR transformation and reengineering during the 1990s. New roles have been created around partnering approaches for HR. Many transactional practices have been outsourced, and some are now being brought back to the inside of leading corporations in shared services. Without these and other breakthrough changes in HR operational capability, people strategies remain largely undelivered.

Kesler and Law (1997) analyzed HR-transformation initiatives in 5 large multinationals and presented a model and process for helping others to learn from those experiences. The research demonstrated that without changes in the 4 key tracks, improvements in the impact of HR functions were limited:

- Role, mission and measures
- Competencies
- Processes and systems
- Structure and role design

Table 4.2 Teams, Partners and Centers

Expert Resource Teams	Front-Line Business Partners	Central Service Centers
• Central pool of specialists/designers • Analyze needs • Benchmark • Develop philosophy and policy with corporate leaders • Design/develop programs • Support roll out of programs; teach others how • Support consultants with "best practices" and key expertise • Ensure best practices are exchanged	• Decentralized, BU aligned "generalists" • Manage client expectations through contracting and execution • Directly support the needs of the business • Create the BU people plan with the line partner • Implement programs; create applications • Manage projects • Accountable to meet the contracted expectations	• Highly consolidated support functions • Manage all "transactional" support systems • Manage systems implementation • Direct projects to eliminate/automate work • Design automated client-focused services • Ensure company standards are met • Conduct diagnostic studies of transactional trends

Companies like Warner-Lambert, Motorola, Coca-Cola and Whirlpool have focused on the need to create new HR-organization structures and to realign roles in order to separate transactional-fulfillment work and consultative, business partnering work. These and other companies have reported significant improvements in delivering strategic results when traditional generalist roles are replaced with more consultative organizational effectiveness roles, supported by a small, centralized team of expert resources and transactional-service providers. Partnering resources are increasingly assigned directly to line business units, while service activities are aggressively consolidated.

While some argue that this work has largely been completed and that companies are now focused on a different agenda for HR, our experience indicates otherwise. The success in building HR functional capability has been greatly overstated, even in published articles, and in any case, remains an ongoing challenge, requiring aggressive attention on a continuous basis (Table 4.2).

Kesler and Law's research identified the need to develop a blueprint for change – a clear change-management plan that overcomes the "vagueness of vision." This action-oriented plan, with a 2–3-year planning horizon, is the fourth critical task in building the strategic HR agenda. The operational plan should be renewed about every 18–24 months. Without the fourth lament in the strategy model, business unit people plans are likely to remain largely unimplemented.

Potential Action Items

- Determine what strengths within the HR function are needed to execute the company-wide objectives and the business unit people plans.
- Conduct a study with line leaders and measure the current extent of those capabilities within the function.

- Define tangible improvement plans across the 4 change tracks.
- Involve large numbers of HR people from across the organization in action-learning workshops to participate in the diagnostic work and to help plan change.
- Charter learning teams to complete specific deliverables.

Completing the HR Strategy Process

The 4-step model provides a practical and thoughtful approach to building a strategic HR agenda for an entire enterprise or a major business sector within a larger company. (In many large corporations, a major sector or region initiates the planning process.)

The strategy outcomes are likely to be greater with high degrees of participation by other HR professionals and line leaders. Necessary degrees of participation vary among the 4 tasks (see Table 4.3).

"HR councils" provide a natural forum for building the HRM agenda. These HR leadership forums, made up of HR heads from various operating units in a given company, are fixtures in most large corporations. While the mission of these groups is nearly always "integration," they often lack an agenda or a clear sense of what integration should look like; members attend meetings month after month, reporting long lists of activities and listening to presentations by technical

Table 4.3   Steps and Participants

Four Steps	Key Owners/Participants
1. Enterprise People Philosophies	CEO/Chief HR Officer
2. Business Unit People Plans	Div. Head/HR Leader
3. Company-Wide HR Priorities	Co.-Wide "HR Leader Council"
4. HR Operations Plan	Co.-Wide "HR Leader Council"

experts. The cross-business HR council in many companies has become a dreaded, low-value adding committee. One sector HR vice president commented, "I attend these meetings, because I know I should. Most of the time, I just hope we can get through the full-day meeting without making any decisions that will add rocks to my wagon, or prevent me from doing something I want to do in my sector."

The 4-step strategy process delivers the value that is added by the cross-company council. At its best, the strategy-setting process is ongoing, and the work is not additive to members' workloads. Instead, it is the channel through which the right things get done by the right people. The elements in the agenda require a longer time for considering collaboration. These working sessions are often facilitated by a third party, so the senior HR officer can participate fully in the content of the dialogue.

With or without a corporate HR council, human resources leaders need to initiate an action-oriented approach to defining a strategic HR agenda in a manner that defines clear roles and relationships among the principal players. They can best do this by involving line leaders in practical, robust dialogue. The 4-step approach provides a road map that carries the dialogue forward.

WHEN MAJOR DIVISIONS INITIATE THE STRATEGY PROCESS

Frequently HR strategy innovation begins within a major division of a large corporation, with or without the support of the senior corporate HR officer. Our experience indicates that a sector or division initiative can work as long as there is an inclusive approach, relative to the corporate functional team.

On numerous occasions, the corporate HR leadership watch the process with interest and often build on the success of a division or sector initiative, deploying a modified form of the process across the enterprise.

When divisions initiate the strategy process, they may involve people at all levels of the business. In one example, a major pharmaceutical division of a large chemical company asked all of its operating sites and major functions to develop "unit people plans" based on the 4-step model. The corporate parent acts more as a holding company and demonstrates little interest in the HR strategy for the enterprise.

Many forms of innovation in large corporations start at the operating unit level. It should be encouraged!

References

Brockbank, W. 1999. If HR were really strategically proactive: Present and future directions in HR's contribution to competitive advantage. *Human Resource Management*, 38(4): 337–350.

Harris, B., Huselid, M. & Becker, B. 1999. Strategic human resource management at Praxair. *Human Resource Management*, 38(4): 316–320.

Huselid, M. A. & Becker, B. E. 1998. High performance work systems, intellectual capital and the creation of shareholder wealth. Working Paper. School of Management and Labor Relations, Rutgers University.

Kesler, G. J. 1996. Unpublished paper prepared for clients.

Kesler, G. & Law, J. 1997. Implementing major change in the HR organisation: The lessons of five companies. *Human Resources Planning*, 20(4): 26–38.

Schuler, R., Fulkerson, J. & Dowling, P. 1991. Strategic performance measurement and management in multinational corporations. *Human Resource Management*, 30: 365–389.

Stalk, G. 1992. Competing on capabilities: The new rules of corporate strategy. *Harvard Business Review*, 70.

Ulrich, D. 1997. *Human Resource Champions: The Next Agenda for Adding Value and Delivering Results*. Boston, MA: Harvard Business School Press.

Ulrich, D. 1998. *Delivering Results*. Boston, MA: Harvard Business School Press.

Wysocki, B. 1999. Corporate America confronts the meaning of a core business. *Wall Street Journal*.

Yeung, A. & Brockbank, W. 1995. Reengineering HR through information technology. *Human Resource Planning*, 18(2): 25–37.

Chapter 5

Roles in Strategic HRM

People Development and Team Work

The establishment of positive business objectives within an organization must be accompanied by the clear allocation of responsibilities within the people structure. It is generally accepted that the primary operational responsibility for ensuring that translation of goals takes place in the organization must rest with the management, but true goal translation is impossible without the full co-operation and commitment of all employees. If they are to accept their full share of responsibility, they must be able to participate fully in the making and monitoring of arrangements for achieving the requirements. Some organizations have protocols whereby people – say in a particular unit – meet periodically for discussions. This "total involvement" approach stresses the need for the participation of every individual employee.

The Process of Performance Management

Managers are in control only when they have created a system and a climate in which their subordinates can exercise self-control. Mechanisms may then be created to provide clear performance standards in all areas, backed by appropriate job descriptions and training, to ensure that those standards are achieved. The process of performance management then consists of:

1. Clarifying responsibilities
2. Developing performance indicators and objectives
3. Preparing action plans

Clarifying Responsibilities

If job descriptions have been written in the organization, they may serve as a starting point for clarifying each individual's role. It should be emphasized, however, that these need to be updated and reviewed with each subordinate to ensure their relevancy. The format of job descriptions is not of critical importance, although they must be standardized for a particular organization. They should contain a statement of the overall purpose, reporting relationships, responsibility and priorities. Agreement must be reached on the priorities; for example, often managers or directors expect the major emphasis to be on activities 2, 5, 6 and 7, when the subordinate perceives the critical areas to be 1, 3, 4 and 8.

Organizational problems, which require role clarification, will not be resolved by the introduction of job descriptions alone. Some of the other factors which prevent people from functioning smoothly are:

■ Poor communication of information to other individuals, departments and groups and delayed communication for the information to be useful
■ Lack of understanding of where decisions should be taken or goals should be set

- Low involvement of other individuals, departments or groups in reaching decisions
- Lack of appreciation on the role of other individuals, departments or groups when goals or targets are reached
- Failure to identify and use systems, methods or techniques for specific activities
- Absence of corrective action, following identification of weaknesses and problems
- Lack of recognition of the role of training and follow-up

The important aspect of the methods used to counter these is the impact of team building within each operational group. Each participant must have the opportunity to review their current roles, seek to change those aspects for which they perceive a valid cause and become more involved in those areas where they feel their inputs would have merit.

Developing Performance Indicators and Objectives

Although the responsibilities should clarify what is to be performed, they do not define how well the tasks are expected to be performed. Performance indicators, therefore, are the means by which performance will be evaluated. To be meaningful, they must be:

- Measurable: The indicators must lead to performance objectives which are quantifiable and tangible. Achievements in these areas must be recordable, verifiable and observable. The quantity or quality of the output, time schedules, costs, ratios or percentages would be examples of measurable indicators.
- Relevant: The indicators must serve as a linkage between specific areas of responsibilities and the individual

performance objectives to monitor achievement. They must describe what is the expected role of the position and the critical areas of performance.

■ Important: The indicators need not be defined for every area of responsibility. They should be developed for those activities which have a significant impact on the results of the individual, the department, and the organization.

The establishment of performance objectives provides a clear direction and communication of the expected levels of achievement. The process is a joint one – an interaction between the manager and his/her subordinates. If full commitment on the part of both parties is to be realized, the targets should be negotiated through a "catch-ball" process, in the form of a performance "contact." Once the indicators have been agreed, the specific results desired need to be decided. The greater the participation, the greater the motivation to achieve. Agreed performance objectives should, therefore, contain the following components:

■ Participation developed
■ Challenging but attainable
■ Clear statements of performance expectations
■ Within the individual's scope of control

Participation – An interaction which leads to mutual agreement provides good exchange of ideas between the manager and his/her subordinates. The results of the interaction should not be a compromise but should be the outcome of a persuasive but logical presentation of why such an outcome is plausible. Discussions should be analytical, not emotional, and deal with both sides of an issue if there are significant differences. The crucial factors in examining the advantages of this approach are:

Involvement – Commitment – Personal responsibility –
Higher drive to achieve
Rather than,
Imposition – Lack of acceptance – External responsibility –
Lower drive to achieve

Challenge – A well-set performance objective is one which
is attainable and yet requires stretching. The achiever sets
targets, which involve a moderate risk. When the likelihood
of success is 65–85%, the inner sense of the challenge is at
its peak. As this probability decreases or increases from this
range, the motive to achieve is reduced. The former makes the
risk too great, since the target becomes perceived as unreal-
istic and self-esteem is lowered. The latter sets the risk as too
low and if success is "guaranteed," the payoff value attached to
attainment is reduced.

When individuals press for objectives that are either too
low or too high, they tend to be motivated more by the fear
of failure than the need to achieve. Those in this category
either want the target to be fail-safe and, hence, be assured of
success or else want to set a target so high that no one really
takes their goals seriously.

To deal most effectively with either of these personalities,
the performance objectives which are established should be of
three levels: minimally acceptable, above average and excellent. A person need not negotiate the minimal acceptable level
since this is the least level of performance to maintain employment. The other levels can be discussed to arrive at realistic,
but challenging, targets. Once these have been agreed upon,
the choice of which path to follow is that of the subordinate,
and the rewards can be similarly distributed.

Clarity of expectation – The target should be objec-
tively expressed and be tied to a specific time framework.
Expressions such as "approximate, minimum, maximum,
adequate, none, as soon as possible" are vague and should

be avoided. Descriptive, evaluative terms such as "frequently, seldom, usually" are also open to misinterpretation.

Scope of control – The performance of the responsibility must be within the limits of authority that have been delegated. An individual cannot be reasonably held responsible for activities that cannot be directly controlled or influenced. For example, a production manager's performance objective of reviewing and accounting for the variation between budgeted and actual performance by the fifth working day of the month may not be adequately expressed, since the input for review may originate in data processing or accounting, rather than the manager's own department. If this is so, he/she may have no control over the budgeting data being available in time for a review on that date. A better indicator might be the time from receipt of the input to the submission of the analysis and the recommendation.

Preparing Action Plans

It is clear that some form of action plan, perhaps in the form of a flow chart, bar chart or Gantt chart, is required to enable the objectives to be reached. The plans should stipulate action by the individuals concerned and be reviewed periodically against the milestones set down. For example,

- How will contributions made by individuals in team projects be evaluated?
- What action will be required to improve job performance?
- What are the criteria for promotion?
- What are the training needs to improve performance or prepare for promotion?
- What are the changes in the goals for the next performance period?

In order to effectively manage performance, an organization must have a performance management system for all its levels. The true translation of goals from the top to the bottom of the organization requires that one level's "hows" become the next level's "whats." This interlocking or goal translation process should ensure that the whole organization is working toward the same achievable mission, as was previously discussed in Chapter 3.

The Need for Teamwork

The complexity of most of the processes operated in the industrial, commercial and the services sectors place them beyond the control of any one individual. The only efficient way to tackle process improvement or problems is through the use of some form of teamwork. The use of the team approach for improvement has many advantages over allowing individuals to work separately:

■ A greater variety of complex issues may be tackled, which are beyond the capability of any one individual or even one department, by the pooling of expertise and resources.
■ Problems are exposed to a greater diversity of knowledge, skill and experience and are solved more efficiently.
■ The approach is more satisfying to team members and boosts morale and ownership through participation in decision-making.
■ Improvement opportunities which cross departmental or functional boundaries can be addressed more easily, and the potential/actual conflicts are more likely to be identified and solved.
■ The recommendations are more likely to be implemented than individual suggestions as the quality of decision-making in a good team is high.

Most of these factors rely on the premise that people are most willing to support any effort in which they have taken part or helped to develop.

When properly managed and developed, teams improve processes, producing results quickly and economically. Teamwork throughout any organization is an essential component of total organizational excellence for it builds trust, improves communications and develops interdependence. Much of what has been taught previously in management has led to a culture in the West of independence, with little sharing of ideas and information. Knowledge is very much like organic manure: if it is spread around, it will fertilize and encourage growth; if it is kept closed inside, it will eventually fester and rot.

Teamwork devoted to process improvement changes independence to interdependence through improved communication, trust and the free exchange of ideas, knowledge, data and information. The use of the face-to-face interaction method of communication, with a common goal, develops over time the sense of dependence on each other. This forms a key part of any improvement process and provides a methodology for employee recognition and involvement through active encouragement in group activities.

Teamwork provides an environment in which people can grow and use all the resources effectively and efficiently to make continuous improvements. As individuals grow, the organization grows. It is worth pointing out, however, that employees will not be motivated toward continual improvement in the absence of:

- Commitment from the top management
- The right organizational "climate"
- A mechanism for enabling individual contributions to be effective

All these are focused essentially on enabling people to feel, accept and discharge responsibility. More than one organization has made this as part of their strategy – to "empower people to act." If one hears from employees comments such as "We know this is not the best way to do this job, but if that is the way the management wants us to do it, that is the way we will do it," then it is clear that the expertise which exists at the point of operation has not been harnessed, and the people do not feel responsible for the outcome of their actions. Responsibility and accountability foster pride, job satisfaction and better work.

Empowerment to act is very easy to express conceptually, but it requires real effort and commitment on the part of all managers and supervisors to put it into practice. Recognition is only partially successful, but good ideas or attempts are to be applauded and not criticized, which is a good way to start. Encouragement of ideas and suggestions from the workforce, particularly through their involvement in team or group activities, requires investment. The rewards are total involvement, both inside the organization and outside through the supplier and customer chains.

Teamwork for process improvement has several components. It is driven by a strategy, needs a structure and must be implemented thoughtfully and effectively. The strategy, which drives the improvement of the teams at various levels, was outlined in Chapter 3, but in essence it comprises:

■ The mission of the organization
■ The critical success factors with key performance indicators
■ The core processes

The structure of having the top management team in a steering committee, and the core process being owned by process teams which manage improvement projects, requires some attention to be given to what makes people work well together and what constitutes inspirational leadership.

Action-Centered Leadership

During the 1960s, John Adair was Senior Lecturer in military history and the Leadership Training Advisor at the Military Academy, Sand Hurst, UK. Later, as Assistant Director of the Industrial Society, he developed what he called the action-centered leadership model, based on his experiences at Sand Hurst, where he had the responsibility to ensure that results in cadet training did not fall below a certain standard. He had observed that some instructors frequently achieved well above average results due to their own natural ability with groups and their enthusiasm. He developed this further into a team model which is the basis for the approach of the author and his colleagues to this subject.

In developing this model for teamwork and leadership, John Adair understood that for any group or team, big or small, to respond to leadership, they need a clearly defined task, and the response and achievement of that task is inter-related to the needs of the team and the separate needs of the individual members of the team. The value of the overlapping circles is that it emphasizes the unity of leadership and the interdependence and multifunctional reaction to single decisions affecting any of the 3 areas.

Leadership Tasks

Drawing upon the discipline of social psychology, John Adair developed and applied to training the functional view of leadership. The essence of this he distilled into the 3 interrelated but distinctive requirements of a leader. These are to define and achieve the job or task, to build and coordinate a team to do this and to develop and satisfy the individuals within the team.

- Task needs – The difference between a team and a random crowd is that a team has some common purpose, goal or objective, e.g., a football team. If a work team does not achieve the required results or meaningful results, it will become frustrated. Organizations have a task: to make a profit, to provide a service or even to survive. So anyone who manages others has to achieve results: production, marketing, selling or whatever. Achieving objectives is a major criterion for success.
- Team needs – To achieve these objectives, the group needs to be held together. People need to be working in a coordinated fashion in the same direction. Teamwork will ensure that the team's contribution is greater than the sum of its parts. Conflict within the team must be used effectively; arguments can lead to ideas or to tension and lack of cooperation.
- Individual needs – Within working groups, individuals also have their own set of needs. They need to know what their responsibilities are, how they will be needed and how well they are performing. They need an opportunity to show their potential, take on responsibility and receive recognition for good work.

The task, team and individual functions for the leader are as follows:

Task functions – Defining the task

- Making a plan
- Allocating work and resources
- Controlling quality and the tempo of work
- Checking performance against the plan
- Adjusting the plan

Team functions – Setting standards

■ Maintaining discipline
■ Building team spirit
■ Encouraging, motivating and giving a sense of purpose
■ Appointing sub-leaders
■ Ensuring communication within the group
■ Training the group

Individual functions – Attending to personal problems

■ Praising individuals
■ Giving the status
■ Recognizing and using individual abilities
■ Training the individual

The team leader's or facilitator's task is to concentrate on the small, central area where all 3 circles overlap – the "action to change" area. In this area, the facilitator's or leader's task is to try to satisfy all 3 areas of need by achieving the task, building the team, and satisfying individual needs. If a leader concentrates only on the tasks, e.g., in going all out for production schedules, while neglecting the training, encouragement and motivation of the team and individuals, he/she may do very well in the short term. Eventually, however, the team members will give less results than they are actually capable of. Similarly, a leader, who concentrates on only creating team spirit, while neglecting the task and the individuals, will not receive maximum contribution from the people. They may enjoy working on the team, but they will lack the real sense of achievement which comes from accomplishing a task to the utmost of their collective ability.

So the leader/facilitator must try to achieve a balance by acing in all 3 areas of overlapping needs. It is always wise to work out a list of required functions within the context of any given situation, based on a general agreement on the essentials. Here is Adair's original Sand Hurst list which may be customized to suit one's context.

■ Planning, e.g., seeking all the available information

Defining group task, purpose or goal
Making a workable plan (in the right decision-making framework)

■ Initiating, e.g., briefing the group on the aims and the plan

Explaining why the aim or the plan is necessary
Allocating tasks to group members
Setting group standards

■ Controlling, e.g., maintaining group standards

Influencing tempo
Ensuring that all actions are taken toward the objectives
Keeping the discussion relevant
Prodding the group to action/decision

■ Supporting, e.g., expressing acceptance of persons and their contributions

Encouraging group/individuals
Disciplining group/individuals
Creating team spirit
Relieving tension with humor
Reconciling disagreements or getting others to explore them

■ Informing, e.g., clarifying the task and the plan

Giving new information to the group, i.e., keeping them "in the picture"
Receiving information from the group
Summarizing suggestions and ideas coherently

■ Evaluating, e.g., checking the feasibility of an idea

Testing the consequences of a proposed solution
Evaluating group performance
Helping the group to evaluate its own performance against the standards

A checklist is given which should assist the team leader to measure the progress against the required functions of fulfilling the task, maintaining the team and growing the people.

Team Processes

The team process is like any other process; it has inputs and outputs. High-performing teams have three main attributes: high task fulfillment, high team maintenance and low self-orientation. These may be subdivided further:

Stages of Team Development

Original work by Tuckman suggested that when teams are put together there are 4 main stages of team development, the so-called forming (awareness), storming (conflict), naming (cooperation) and performing (productivity). The characteristics of each stage and some key aspects to look out for in the early stages are given below.

Clear Objectives and Agreed Performance Goals

No group of people can be effective unless they know what they want to achieve, but it is more than knowing what the objectives are. People are only likely to be committed to them if they can identify with and have ownership of them; in other words, objectives and performance goals are agreed by team members. Often this agreement is difficult to achieve, but experience shows that it is an essential prerequisite for an effective group.

Openness and Confrontation

If a team is to be effective, then the members of the team need to be able to state their views, their differences of opinion as well as their interests and problems without fear of ridicule or retaliation. No teams work effectively if there is a cutthroat atmosphere, where members become less willing or able to express themselves openly, and much energy, effort and creativity is lost.

Support and Trust

Support naturally implies trust among team members. Where individual group members do not feel they have to protect their territory or job and feel able to talk straight to other members – about both "nice" and nasty things – then the opportunity exists for trust to be shown. Based on this trust, people can talk freely about their fears and problems and receive from others the help they need to be more effective.

Cooperation and Conflict

When there is an atmosphere of trust, members are more ready to be involved and committed. Information is shared rather than hidden. Individuals listen to the ideas of others and build on them. People find ways of being more helpful to each other and the group generally. Cooperation causes high morale – individuals accept each other's strengths and weaknesses and contribute from their pool of knowledge and skill. All abilities, knowledge and experience are fully utilized by the group; individuals have no inhibitions about using other people's abilities to help solve their problems, which are shared.

Allied to this, conflicts are seen as a necessary and useful part of organizational life. An effective team works through issues of conflict and uses the results to help achieve objectives. Conflict prevents teams from becoming complacent and lazy and often they generate new ideas.

Good Decision-Making

As mentioned earlier, objectives need to be clearly and completely understood by all members before good decision-making can commence. In making decisions effective, teams develop the ability to collect information quickly, and then discuss the alternatives openly. They become committed to their decisions and ensure action quickly.

Appropriate Leadership

Effective teams have a leader whose responsibility is to achieve results through the efforts of a number of people. Power and authority can be applied in many ways, and team members often differ on the style of leadership they prefer. Collectively, teams may agree on different views of leadership, but, whatever their view, an effective team usually sorts through the alternatives in an open and honest way.

Review of the Team Process

Effective teams understand not only the groups character and its role in the organization, but how it makes decisions, deals with conflicts, etc. The team process allows the team to learn from experiences and to consciously improve teamwork. There are numerous ways of looking at team processes – by using an observer, by a team member giving feedback or by the whole group discussing their performance.

Sound Inter-Group Relationships

No human being or group is an island; they need the help of others. An organization will not achieve maximum benefit from a collection of improvement teams which are effective within themselves, but which fight with each other.

Individual Development Opportunities

High-performance teams seek to pool the skills of individuals, and it necessarily follows that they pay attention to the development of individual skills and try to provide opportunities to individuals to grow and learn and, of course, have fun.

Strategic HR plays a critical role in the organization to make it the most respected company in the country and in the world.

Strategic HR helps the organization to imbibe the concept of tangible and intangible growth through the vision and values of the organization. It helps to create value for the customer by building an organization where people feel excited to work and also be a good corporate citizen.

Therefore, many respected companies, as listed under the Top 25 Companies in India below, have carved out a strategic role for HR functions in scoring on the below parameters.

1. Overall quality
2. Quality of the top management
3. Depth and quality of talent
4. Ability to attract and retain talent
5. Belief in transparency
6. Ethics
7. Social responsibility
8. Environmental consciousness
9. Quality of products/services

10. Response to customer needs
11. Corporate/product brand management
12. Dynamism
13. Speed of response to change
14. Belief in innovation
15. Global competitiveness
16. Consistent performance
17. Returns to shareholder
18. Global competitiveness
19. Consistent performance
20. Returns to shareholder
21. Value creation for stakeholders
22. Ability to cope with recession

Top 25 Companies in India

1. Infosys Technologies
2. Reliance Industries
3. Wipro
4. Hindustan Lever
5. Maruti Udyog
6. Dr. Reddy's Laboratories
7. HDFC Bank
8. Jet Airways
9. ICICI Bank
10. Ranbaxy Laboratories
11. GCMMF (Amul)
12. Tata Motors
13. TCS
14. Larsen & Toubro
15. Tata Iron & Steel
16. State Bank of India
17. ONGC

18. Hero Honda Motors
19. Asian Paints (India)
20. Bajaj Auto
21. ITC
22. Indian Oil Corp.
23. Nokia India
24. Citibank
25. LIC

Let's discuss the view of the chief mentor and head of the most respected company in India, Infosys Technologies:

A company that adds an organization equivalent to half its size every year poses a very stiff challenge to those reclusive strategists – the board of directors. When such scorching growth (40% and above) comes on annual revenues of $1 billion plus, the responsibility grows manifold.

For the board of directors, even one that includes the likes of N.R. Narayana Murthy, Nandan Nilekani, Omkar Goswami, Larry Pressler and Claude Smadja, piloting such an organization can be treacherous. A simple error of judgment could spell disaster. So, how do they do justice to the onerous responsibility of defining future strategies without jeopardizing the current rate of growth?

The Infosys Technologies board believes it has found the answer in the 1:1:3 formula. In its offerings to the world, consulting was conspicuous by its absence. The board believes that the $20 million investment in starting the consulting practice, Infosys Consulting Inc., will be pivotal to how Infosys will grow. This is what the formula means: For every single consulting specialist expected to join, Infosys Technologies would place at least 1 person on site and another 3 offshore. The attempt is to create a potent force in the IT industry by manning consulting with global delivery. The Infosys board thinks that if the 1:2:3 strategy can be implemented, it would be possible to piggyback more on the consulting business – that consulting will generate enough downstream work to keep the organization on a high growth path. Infosys's revenues from consulting are at 3.4% today. The company claims it hasn't set a revenue target for Infosys Consulting yet.

Infosys Consulting is being led by CEO Stephen Pratt, former global leader of Deloitte Consulting's customer relationship management (CRM) practice. Its managing directors include Romil Bahl, ex-vice president, consulting services, EDS; Raj Joshi, former CEO of Deloitte Consulting Offshore Technology Group; and Paul Cole, ex-head, global operations, Cap Gemini, Infosys Consulting hired 75 people by March 2005 and 500 consultants by March 2007.

To provide the support structure to 1:1:3, the board took a strategic decision. In November 2003, Infosys restructured itself from geographical business units to fully integrated vertical industry groups called Independent Business (IBUs). The IBUs are banking and capital markets, insurance and healthcare, automotive and aerospace, and retail, distribution and consumer packaged goods (CPG). The board believes that such a structure – most international IT firms are structured this way – will create multiple growth engines within the organization, especially since each IBU head has been fully empowered, like a CEO, to design and implement this strategy.

The 1:1:3 plans will also draw support from the BPO business. While Infosys's BPO subsidiary Progeon lags behind its peers, its board has decided to keep off the call center business. Instead, the company will focus on areas

like business transaction, sales order and financial recon-
ciliation. "Call centers have become a commodity business.
We would like to keep away from it," says Nandan Nilekani,
CEO and MD. Despite that, Infosys's ITES revenues were
expected to double to $34 million in 2009, from $17 million
in 2008.

Next, to monitor targets and for mid-course corrections,
Infosys has a triple-horizon strategic planning model. In
the first horizon, progress will be tracked from a quarter
to a year. In the second horizon, the board will approve a
3-year crystal ball gazing plan to find answers to questions
like Infosys's response if China becomes hugely competitive in IT or if there is shortage of labor in India or the pos-
sibility of a radical technological change and the company's
readiness for such a scenario.

Infosys also has a risk mitigation group to look at a
variety of risks, ranging from micro- and macro-economic
risks to technological and geographical risks as well as
risks in application areas.

Strategies like these have prevented other Indian corpo-
rates from unseating Infosys Technologies from the top slot
in the BW Most Respected Companies list (Infosys has held
the number one position since 2001). After all, dynamic
industries require dynamic planning, and Infosys has more
than proved that it's a veteran at that.

Strategic HRM and Employer Branding

Strategic HRM plays a major and critical role in building the
employer brand. Let's take a look at the corporate world.

The third BT-Hewitt study on best employers in India 2003
is replete with surprises: a new No. 1, a clutch of public sector
companies that make the list, and several stars that have suddenly gone missing.

Rank	Best Employer in India 2003	Total No of Employees	Average Training Hours/Years	Training Budget as a % of Gross Revenue	Attrition Rate (%)	Gross Revenue in Rupees (Crore)	Key Drivers for Attraction and Retention of Talent as Perceived by The Company
1	Procter & Gamble India	650	60 hours	0.0005	0.05	809	• Early responsibility in careers • Flexible and transparent organizational culture • Global opportunities through a variety of exposure and diverse experiences • Performance recognition
2	American Express (India)	914	90 hours	0.25	13	129.4	• Strong global brand • Value-based environment • Pioneers in many people practices
3	National Thermal Power Corporation	23,555	50 hours	0.25	1.12	18,584	• Learning and growth opportunities • Competitive rewards • Opportunity to grow, learn, and implement • Strong social security and employee welfare and performance-oriented culture

(Continued)

Rank	Best Employer in India 2003	Total No of Employees	Average Training Hours/Years	Training Budget as a % of Gross Revenue	Attrition Rate (%)	Gross Revenue in Rupees (Crore)	Key Drivers for Attraction and Retention of Talent as Perceived by The Company
4	Johnson & Johnson	492	95 hours	0.5	5.03	n.a.	• Strong values of trust, caring, fairness, and respect within the organization • Freedom to operate at work • Early responsibility in career • Training and learning opportunities • Visible, transparent, and accessible leaders • Competitive rewards • Innovative HR programs and practices
5	GlaxoSmithKline Consumer Healthcare	2,863	96–224 hours	0.02	7.26	992	• Performance-driven rewards • Organization that believes in "growing our own timber" • Comprehensive development and learning programs • Flat organization, where performance could lead to very quick career progression • Challenging work content • Exhaustive induction and orientation program • Competitive rewards

(Continued)

Rank	Best Employer in India 2003	Total No of Employees	Average Training Hours/Years	Training Budget as a % of Gross Revenue	Attrition Rate (%)	Gross Revenue in Rupees (Crore)	Key Drivers for Attraction and Retention of Talent as Perceived by The Company
6	Tata Steel	44,235	77 hours	0.2	3.4	9,843.66	• Organization philosophy and culture • Job stability • Freedom to work and innovate
7	Colgate-Palmolive India	1,171	16–24 hours	2.51	4.8	1,057	• Company brand • Open, transparent and caring organization • Management accounting for managing according to the guiding principles Training and development programs • Structured career planning process • Global career opportunities
8	Wipro	21,561	100 hours	2.5	7	3,467	• Company's brand as an employer • Early opportunities for growth • High degree of autonomy • Value compatibility • Innovative people programs

(Continued)

Rank	Best Employer in India 2003	Total No of Employees	Average Training Hours/Years	Training Budget as a % of Gross Revenue	Attrition Rate (%)	Gross Revenue in Rupees (Crore)	Key Drivers for Attraction and Retention of Talent as Perceived by The Company
9	Indian Oil Corporation	31,647	40 hours	0.04	0.48	1,14,864	• Company brand image • Work culture • Learning and growth opportunities • Challenging work assignments • Growing organization
10	Tata Consultancy Services	22,416	105 hours	7.5	3.67	5,012	• The group brand equity • Strong corporate governance and citizenship • Commitment to learning and development • Best in class people practices • Challenging assignments • Opportunity to work with Fortune 500 clients
11	MindTree Consulting	595	80 hours	1	7.1	28.45	• Work content • Work culture • Competency development and growth opportunities

(Continued)

Rank	Best Employer in India 2003	Total No of Employees	Average Training Hours/Years	Training Budget as a % of Gross Revenue	Attrition Rate (%)	Gross Revenue in Rupees (Crore)	Key Drivers for Attraction and Retention of Talent as Perceived by The Company
12	STMicroelectronics	1,016	45 hours	n.a.	4	n.a.	• International brand recognition and equity • Unique and open work culture • Promotion of empowerment and initiative • Recognition of achievements • Need-based and focused training in both technical and soft skills • Competitive compensation and benefits policies • Opportunity to work on challenging projects
13	Philips India	2,943	24 hours	1	13	1,618.7	• The company brand • Freedom of working • Recognition of performance • Open and transparent culture • Fair and equal opportunity employer

(Continued)

Rank	Best Employer in India 2003	Total No of Employees	Average Training Hours/Years	Training Budget as a % of Gross Revenue	Attrition Rate (%)	Gross Revenue in Rupees (Crore)	Key Drivers for Attraction and Retention of Talent as Perceived by The Company
14	Bharti Tele-Ventures	4,968	91 hours	0.5	12.81	1,486.2	• Leadership position in the market • Strong employer brand • Robust people practices • Opportunity for individual growth • Strong career development process
15	Tata Motors	22,521	88 hours	0.12	3.57	8,918	• The company brand • High degree of people orientation • High performance, seamless and customer-focused culture • Challenging work intent • Opportunity for cross-functional and location mobility • Focused training designed to meet the needs of high performers
16	Microsoft India	150	40 hours	n.a.	2	n.a.	• Freedom to innovate, develop, adapt and change products used by people world over • Flexibility at workplace to encourage work life balance • Freedom to choose career paths

(Continued)

Rank	Best Employer in India 2003	Total No of Employees	Average Training Hours/Years	Training Budget as a % of Gross Revenue	Attrition Rate (%)	Gross Revenue in Rupees (Crore)	Key Drivers for Attraction and Retention of Talent as Perceived by The Company
17	Bharat Petroleum Corporation	12,543	24 hours	0.5	1.7	42,294	• Organizational culture • Opportunity for high level of exposure • Job security • Healthy relationships at work
18	Eureka Forbes	5,918	96 hours	0.25	29	399	• Unlimited opportunity for earning and learning • Quick and steady rise of the career graph • Fun, excitement and recognition
19	Wipro Spectra mind	4,500	200 hours	1.36	23	52.1	• Career progression opportunities • Open and transparent communication system. • Focus on continuous improvement • High degree of culture consciousness and focus on values • A healthy work life balance

(Continued)

Rank	Best Employer in India 2003	Total No of Employees	Average Training Hours/Years	Training Budget as a % of Gross Revenue	Attrition Rate (%)	Gross Revenue in Rupees (Crore)	Key Drivers for Attraction and Retention of Talent as Perceived by The Company
20	Aditya Birla Group	51,000	33 hours	1	1.14	14,119	• Diversified conglomerate providing multiple career opportunities • Clear future directions for growth • Highly empowering culture
21	E.I. Dupont India	321	56 hours	0.25	2.6	600	• The corporate brand and international exposure • Work environment encouraging work and life balance • Competitive rewards
22	Eli Lilly and Company (I)	530	81 hours	0.5	26	135	• Image of the company • Global career opportunities • Competitive rewards
23	Maruti Udyog	4,600	108 hours	0.5	4	9,410.3	• Openness and continuous learning culture • Performance orientation • Customer obsession across levels • International benchmarks • Complete alignment across the organization

(Continued)

Rank	Best Employer in India 2003	Total No of Employees	Average Training Hours/Years	Training Budget as a % of Gross Revenue	Attrition Rate (%)	Gross Revenue in Rupees (Crore)	Key Drivers for Attraction and Retention of Talent as Perceived by The Company
24	Larsen & Toubro	22,000	19 hours	1.4	9.5	9,869.83	• Corporate reputation • Opportunity to learn • Freedom of operation • Fair employment practices
25	Monsanto India	362	15 hours	1	9.7	333.4	• Informal culture • Empowered workplace • Focus on organizational values • Industry leader • Challenging careers • Employee-oriented environment and policies • Learning and development opportunities

WHAT MAKES 'EM ROCK

They view talent management as an important investment, not cost.

They focus on building a high-performance work environment.

They clearly articulate the elements of their organization's culture.

They use rewards as a differentiating tool and build leaders at all levels.

References

Becker, B. E. & Huselid, M. A. 1998. High performance work systems and firm performance: A synthesis of research and managerial implications. *Research in Personnel and Human Resource Management*, 16: 53–101.

Becker, B. E., Huselid, M. A. & Ulrich, D. 2001. *The HR Scorecard: Linking People, Strategy and Performance*. Boston, MA: Harvard Business School Press.

Boudreau, J. W. & Ramstad, P. M. 1999. Human resource metrics: Can measures be strategic? *Research in Personnel and Human Resources Management, Supplement*, 4: 75–98.

Boudreau, J. W. & Ramstad, P. M. 2001. Supply-chain measurement for staffing. Working Paper 01-16. Ithaca, NY: Center for Advanced Human Resource Studies, Cornell University.

Boudreau, J. W. & Ramstad, P. M. 2002. From "professional business partner" to "strategic talent leader": "What's next" for human resource management. Working Paper 02-10. Ithaca, NY: Center for Advanced Human Resource Studies, Cornell University.

Boudreau, J. W. & Ramstad, P. M. in press. Strategic I/O psychology and the role of utility analysis models. In: W. Borman, R. Klimoski & D. Ilgen (Eds.), *Handbook of Industrial and Organizational Psychology*. New York, NY: Wiley.

Boudreau, J. W., Dunford, B. B. & Ramstad, P. 2001. The human capital "impact" on e-business: The case of encyclopedia Britannica. In: N. Pal & J. M. Ray (Eds.), *Pushing the Digital Frontier: Insights into the Changing Landscape of e-Business.* New York, NY: AMACOM.

Brookings Institute. 2000. Understanding intangible sources of value: Human capital sub group report [online]. http://www.brook.edu/es/research/projects/intangibles/doc/sub_hcap.htm.

Cappelli, P. & Neumark, D. 2001. Do "high-performance" work practices improve establishment-level outcomes? *Industrial and Labor Relations Review,* 54(4): 737–775.

Fitz-enz, J. 1995. *How to Measure Human Resources Management.* New York, NY: McGraw-Hill.

Gerhart, B. A., Wright, P. M., McMahan, G. C. & Snell, S. 2000. Measurement error in research on human resources and firm performance: How much error is there and how does it influence effect size estimates? *Personnel Psychology,* 53(4): 803–834.

Kaplan, R. S. & Norton, D. P. 1996. Using the balanced scorecard as a strategic management system. *Harvard Business Review,* 75–85.

Lepak, D. P. & Snell, S. A. 1999. The human resource architecture: Toward a theory of human capital allocation and development. *The Academy of Management Review,* 24(1): 34–48.

Pfau, B. & Kay, I. 2002. *The Human Capital Edge: 21 People Management Practices Your Company Must Implement (Or Avoid) to Maximize Shareholder Value.* New York, NY: McGraw-Hill.

Rucci, A. J., Kirn, S. P. & Quinn, R. T. 1998. The employee-customer-profit chain at Sears. *Harvard Business Review,* January–February 1998, 83–97.

Shelgren, D. 2001. HR outsourcing. *The Journal of Business Strategy,* 22(4): 4.

Tichy, N. 1998. The teachable point of view. *Journal of Business Strategy,* January–February 1998.

Walker, G. & MacDonald J. R. 2001. Designing and implementing an HR Scorecard. *Human Resource Management,* 40(4): 365–377.

Chapter 6

Improving Business Performance through Strategic HRM

The Best and the Rest

Sifting through the qualitative and quantitative data of 220 organizations that participated in the survey in 2007 revealed several things. For starters, the best employers have more engaged employees – 76% compared to 62% of the rest. But make no mistake. Engaged does not mean either satisfied or committed. There is a big, fundamental difference between being engaged and being merely satisfied or committed, and it often means the difference between an organization's success and failure.

Engaged employees, as the survey found out, speak positively about their company, have a desire to be part of its future and contribute effectively toward its success. Satisfaction, on the other hand, is merely a reflection of how much people like working in an organization. Commitment is a measure of how much they want to contribute to its success. But engagement is a barometer of how much employees want to and how much they actually do to improve business results. Therefore, the higher the employee engagement, the better the organization's performance.

Typically, there are 6 drivers of employee engagement. These are people, work, opportunities, quality of life, procedures and compensation. The people part is about senior leadership, coworkers, culture and values. Work is about motivation, nature of the work and the availability and quality of resources. Opportunities reflect career growth, training and recognition. Procedures are the policies and HR. Pay, benefits and rewards are part of the compensation driver, while quality of life is very obviously about the balance between personal life and work.

These 6 drivers impact engagement either positively or negatively, but all allow prioritization for a higher investment return. The driver with the highest potential of positive impact on employee engagement in India – where the best employer engagement level at 76% is lower than Asia's 90%, – is career opportunities, which is the employee's perception of personal and professional development opportunities within the organization. The driver with the highest potential of negative impact on employee engagement is intrinsic motivation, which is the value employees derive from their work and how they feel about this value.

The question therefore is, what is it that the best employers do that heightens their employee engagement? The study throws up 5 broad themes that are in common. They view talent management as an important investment; they proactively create a high-performance work environment; they clearly sell out their organizational culture; they use rewards as a differentiating tool; and they develop leaders at all levels of the organization. For example, the CEOs of the best employers spend an average of 56% of their time on people-related issues such as development and learning, compared to 40% of the non-best. A high 84% of the best have a succession and replacement planning versus 67% of the rest. Here are some more suggestions based on the data from the best employers.

Best Practices

1. Senior leadership's commitment to employees

   a. CEO communicates business information to employees
   b. Uses employee surveys
   c. Uses formal programs to encourage suggestions

2. Commitment to employee learning and development

   a. Offer multiple and formal career-planning mechanisms
   b. Offer mentoring
   c. Offer tuition reimbursement
   d. Median hours of training required

3. Adherence to strong values

   a. Use "fit" as a key selection criterion
   b. Emphasize acculturation in orientation
   c. Keep consistent practices across the organization

4. Engaging employees in the business

   a. Employees have the opportunity to evaluate managers
   b. Offer job rotation opportunities
   c. Offer broad-base ownership opportunities

5. Paying close attention to employees' quality of life

   a. Offer flextime
   b. Offer reduced hour opportunities
   c. Maternity leave beyond the specified limit and disability plans
   d. Child-care discounts

"Engaged employees have the desire to be part of the company in the future and contribute effectively toward its success."

This survey has highlighted the analysis it made the following way:

- 96% offer job enrichment or redesign compared to 77% of the rest.
- 82% view talent management as a CEO's, and not HR, agenda (vs. 53% of the rest).
- 88% of the CEOs felt that their managers understand their organization's key performance measures (vs. 77% of the rest).
- 96% consult people broadly before implementing major organizational changes (vs. 83% of the rest).
- 24% pay more than 3 times differential in increment between a high performer and an average performer (vs. 17% of the rest).
- 82% of the employees have complete confidence in the integrity of their leaders in their organizations (vs. 73% of the rest).
- 44% provide broad-based stock options to encourage ownership among employees (vs. 16% of the rest).

There are many other attributes common to the best employers. These include focus on multidimensional development rather than only training, faster hiring-cycle time, multiple staffing strategies and more rigorous staffing practices, emphasis on culture and values and their alignment to organizational programs, the use of a variety of compensation components to share the company's financial success and development of organizational leaders from within rather than through lateral recruitment. But here's the most surprising bit: The best employers are not necessarily the best paymasters. In fact, in most cases, they only pay marginally better. That said, we also found that the best paid better than the rest at the junior management level. Even a public sector unit such as the Indian Oil Corporation pays its officer trainees Rs. 6 lakhs per annum.

Becoming the Best: Lessons from around the Globe

For the past 4 years, Hewitt Associates has periodically been conducting "Best Employers" studies across the globe. Covering 1,200 organizations in Asia-Pacific, Australia, Brazil, Canada, India and Europe, these studies have yielded rich insights into what makes the best employer, be it India or the US. Apparently, 80% of the factors that go into the making of the best employer in one country are also the same factors that make another one in another country. For example, there seems to be consensus among the employees of best employers that the factors that have the highest impact on their engagement are relationship with the immediate supervisor, development opportunities, work-life balance and rewards and recognition. The senior leadership, on its part, is committed to employees, encouraging interaction and investing time in addressing people's issues and concerns. It also adheres to strong values, creating a positive organizational culture.

So, Is there a "magic formula" for becoming the best employer? No. But going by the evidence from the best employers in India and elsewhere, there does seem to be a route to becoming one. And that route starts with the top leadership committing itself to the goal of becoming the best employer. Then, it must attract people who are not just talented but fit in with the organization's values and aim for complete employee engagement. That done, it must align people management practices to create the right environment. Finally, the organization must measure the impact and keep at it. If not, fix it and go again.

Does being the best employer pay? You bet. As Hewitt's global studies reveal, best employers have a lower employee turnover. In the United States, best employers have half the churn compared to others; in India it is 45% lower. Best employers also attract a larger pool of talent, and their performance on stock markets is better. In India, best employers outperform comparable indices and industry-related performance metrics by 15%. Besides, best employers have better organizational morale.

The bottom-line, as it emerges, is that being the best employer is not merely an HR issue. It's a strategic issue best championed by the CEO himself. For he's not just the chief employer, but the most important employee too.

Designing the Role of Corporate HR with a Focus on Strategic HRM

The Changing Profile of HRM – Traditional and Strategic HR

Traditional HR	Strategic HR
• HR planning	• Strategic HR planning
• Advisory	• Business strategic/business partner
• Training and development	• Proactive
• Labor relation	• Employee advocate
• Administrator	• Change agent
• Recruitment and selection	
• Welfare and working condition	• Facilitative
• Performance management linked to compensation	• Professional development
• Employee grievance • Salary and wage administration • Maintenance of records	• Problem solver and consultant
• Performance management	• Total quality management

(*Continued*)

Traditional HR	Strategic HR
• Rewards and recognition	• Lead with example
• Reactive	• Resource and productivity manager
• Control oriented	• Cultural awareness (transforming culture: merger and acquisition)
• Quick fix – problem fixer	• HR functional experts-expertise factor • Selection and retention of quality manpower • Performance management – developmental angle

The Changing Profile of HRM – Competency

Competency	It Means
• Able to build trust relationship • Integrity/honesty	• Confidence and secrecy of confidential information • Gain trust and confidence • No favoritism • Respect others (seniors and juniors.)
• Able to influence • Leadership	• Motivate others to participate • Ability to encourage new ideas • Creativity • Punctuality • Team participation to achieve organizational goals
• Able to make decisions • Decision-making	• Logical decision • Listen to different opinions • Timely and thoughtful decisions • Risk-taking ability • Impact of decisions on the customer and the organization

(*Continued*)

114 Strategic Human Resource Management

Competency	It Means
• Teamwork	• Work effectively as a team leader or team member • Sharing nature • To reach a consensus • Understand others and achieve team and mutual goals
• Analytical ability • Reasoning	• Analyze the multiplicity of data and information • Arrive at a logical conclusion • Result oriented
• Knows HR laws and policies • Legal government and jurisprudence	• Keep current records • Understand statutory and regulatory requirements
• Manages conflict • Problem solving	• Initiate in solving or helping to solve the problem • Analyze origin of the problem and again analyze the measurable steps • Solution to compensation, staffing, performance management and training and development
• Knows staff, line roles and the customer • Organization awareness	• Understand the HR role within the organization • Understand delegation of authority • Purpose of the organization • Sensitive to needs and concerns
• Knows individual team behavior	• Apply the knowledge of individual and team behavior to achieve organizational goals • Performance management techniques • Dispute resolution approach to enable the organization to optimize human performance in support of the mission, goal and values.

(Continued)

Competency	It Means
• Knows, applies and manages best practices for maximizing human potential	• Use techniques to measure the HR program and individual HR professional's performance
• Technical competency, learning and teaching others	• Encourage and recommend colleagues toward developmental opportunities for gaining professional experience in as many HR areas as possible • Formal and informal techniques of staff development • Ability to serve the lowest-level employees and lowest-level supervisor of an organization
• Communication skills • Oral and written communication	• Express ideas and exchange information • Share information with staff and the line manager • Communicate effectively with all levels of the organization • Deliver information effectively • Minimizing complex and bureaucratic language
• Able to design and use survey to obtain feedback from customers • Information	• Know and use data collection tools • To develop a new survey or redesign a survey to meet specific data gathering needs or tailor the format to a specific issue
• Use consensus building skills	• Negotiating and influencing • Consultation and negotiation skills • Conflict management (managing conflict) • Managing a diverse workforce

The Changing Profile of HRM – Role and Tools/Systems

Role	It Means	Tools/Systems
• Strategist	• HR practitioner craft and implement long-term plans of the HR function and policies to align the HR function to the business strategy	• HR planning, training and development • Empowerment • Communication • Coordination • Decision-making • Retention management • Delegation of authority • Recruit high-quality professionals • Commitment and trust • Linking HR with the business strategy • Motivation • Employee welfare and benefit
• Integrator	• Link the efforts to those of the whole organization and build consensus	• Communication • Coordination • Proper networking • Manage conflict • Information technology • Good people relations • Increase teamwork • Increase morale
• Business partner	• HR practitioner works closely with top management and key line manager has to ensure that the work environment is inductive to achieving high performance in the right direction, i.e., business goal/ vision.	• Promote teamwork • Communicate well • Training and Development • Job redesign • Performance management • Dispute/conflict resolution • Trust and faith • Sense of accountability and sense of urgency

(*Continued*)

Role	It Means	Tools/Systems
• Problem solving and consultant	• Proactively eliminates the root cause of the performance problem and seizes the competitive advantage or handles the problems which are a hinderance in bringing the best out of people	• Build credibility • Redesign and reposition jobs • Training and development • Rewards and recognition • Coaching and feedback • Counseling
• Change agent	• To facilitate the change process which is least painful and acceptable in the desired direction	• New system

The benefits of the Corporate HR is that it facilitates departments in dealing with their people-related issues in the most effective way and guides and assists them in utilizing the human resources of the organizations, Corporate HR mainly suggests and the unit HR implements the ideas to achieve the organizational goals in a more effective way (Figure 6.1).

Notes Based on Discussions with the HR Head of SRF

■ The role of Corporate HR is important because they believe that it provides the overall mission of the organization so that employees can have a wider perception of organizational beliefs, which would help them in better understanding the organization's policies and practices so that they can do their job in a better way; according to them it also helps in vertically integrating all the functions to achieve organizational goals.

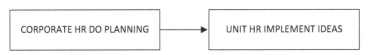

CORPORATE HR DO PLANNING ⟶ UNIT HR IMPLEMENT IDEAS

Figure 6.1   From macro HR to micro HR.

■ The objectives of Corporate HR are to provide:

   a) Strategic direction
   b) Strategic focus so that it can lead to overall organizational growth.

■ The benefits of a well-defined, systematic role of the Corporate HR is that basically it is a central agency through which the organization can coordinate all HR activities to achieve organizational goals. It also helps in benchmarking the organization's HR practices with the best HR practices of an organization in any part of the world for:

   a) Improvement in the current HR practices
   b) Face competition by improving the functioning of the overall organization

The role of the Corporate HR also helps us in:

a) Employee development
b) Competency building
c) Launching the product
d) Joint venture

Thus the Corporate HR plays the role of a coach as well as a service role and a strategic role.

■ One of the negative aspects of the Corporate HR is that it is sometimes engaged in operational day-to-day activities of the organization, but the unit HR departments should take care of these operational activities.
■ Regarding the relationship of the Corporate HR with the unit HR, it provides information regarding what is

Figure 6.2 HR feedback loop.

happening at the plant level, and then the Corporate HR does the planning of the policies and practices which are implemented by the unit HR, which again provides feedback regarding the policies and practices implemented.

Modifications in planning according to the Corporate HR people of SRF should be done by both the doer and the thinker, that is by both the unit HR and the Corporate HR and only then it will be effective.

By planning the activities, the Corporate HR becomes the connecting link between the unit HR people and the larger group (Figure 6.2).

■ Regarding societal and governmental obligations in SRF, they have a "Corporate Services Department" which is handled by a VP-level person and which looks after many schools and other key areas of social welfare. Here the Corporate HR is not the right forum, but still they provide help by suggesting ideas where needed.
■ Key result areas help the organization to realize its potential and there are benefits associated with its development. The key result areas are worked out by the meeting of the MD with other departmental heads, which is:

Employee satisfaction which may be by either:

a) Career development, or
b) Better compensation

They realized that at the junior-level compensation is more important, whereas at the senior level it is a basket of benefits which is more important to employees, but different people have different sets of values, beliefs, perceptions, etc., and in this regard the role of the Corporate HR should be such so that it helps people agreeing on a common policy.

1. Regarding the talent pool in the organization, for the employees to be able adapt themselves to different countries, the organization has trained people in Dubai who can go to any part of the world and can act according to the circumstances of that region. They can also adapt to the culture of that region and their way of practice.
2. For training and development, the Corporate HR designs and creates the system, and the different departmental heads monitor it. They believe that training regarding knowledge and skill should be provided at the departmental level, whereas training regarding behavior and attitude should be provided at the Corporate HR level.
3. For recruitment and selection, the role of Corporate HR is mainly either at the senior level or at the entry level because they believe that these people are going to define the future functioning of the organization because the quality of the plant depends on the quality of the seeds and so here the role of the Corporate HR is very much important.
4. Regarding the compensation and benefits, it is decided on the basis of the performance system and on the grade and role performed by an employee.
5. Regarding career growth and development, the organization has very clear guidelines on how it identifies the person to be promoted and provides them the right opportunity to grow with the organization's various methods according to the opportunities available in the organization.

6. For communication within the organization, they have a news magazine "STRIDES" which is published every 2 months.
7. One important factor they shared with us is that there is very high employee involvement within the organization that leads to high employee satisfaction. Employees in the organization have rated role clarity and facility high, but compensation was rated low by the employees.
8. The president of the organization heads total quality management, and the Corporate HR does not play any major role in that.
9. Competencies required for the Corporate HR employee are as follows:
   a) Knowledge
      • Knowledge of the overall business process
      • Understanding of the international benchmark
      • Understanding of different HR systems worldwide
      • Good knowledge of HR practices in the Indian industry
      • Knowledge of industrial and legal laws
   b) Skills
      • Good communication and implementation skills
      • Skills to build a consensus and facilitative process
      • Presentation skills
      • Appraisal skills
      • Interpersonal skills
      • Network skills
   c) Attitude
      • Role model
      • Leader
   d) Behavior
      • Sensitive to human feelings
      • Trustworthy and caring
      • Empathy
10. The organization also has a performance support system which facilitates and guides employees to perform better,

and they also reward and recognize their employees' performance and so in this way the Corporate HR motivates them to perform better.

Notes Based on Discussions with the Regional HR Manager of SBCH

Corporate HR plays a very strategic role because they have a) Three plants, b) Three contract manufacturing sites, c) Seven packaging sites and a large number of depots.

Employees work at different locations, and to coordinate all the people-related issues of these different locations from one place and bring about uniformity among these policies and practices, there arises the need for the Corporate HR, which acts as a central hub for all the operations. The Corporate HR aligns all the human elements of the organization in such a way that it helps the organization in achieving goals through its people.

One important information in this regard is that it sets goals for the organization; for example, if they set a goal for the organization to achieve something in 10 years, then they divide it for 3 years and again they would divide it to achieve the goal in parts within 1 year so that finally these acts are added up, which help the organization to achieve its goal finally.

Corporate HR provides the support to different plant managers and regional managers in dealing with people-related issues of the organization.

1. Benefits of the Corporate HR: It helps the organization in formulating and implementing uniform policies and practices throughout the organization so that every employee in the organization would talk one language regarding the policies and practices of the organization and all of them would feel equal in terms of the treatment meted

out by the organization. They also help the organization as a business partner by coordinatng with all the human elements of the organization to achieve its goal within the different departments.

2. The function of the Corporate HR with the unit HR people: They empower their unit HR people in such a way and delegate authority to them in such a manner that they deal with labor-related problems of the organization in an effective manner and take important actions and decisions.

    Corporate HR mainly plays an advisory role in this regard, and if they feel it is necessary, they provide suggestions and advice to the unit HR people on problems related to labor.

3. SBCH as an organization is very much committed to societal and governmental obligations, and wherever they have plants or offices they are very much committed to their social obligations that they maintain bus stops, greenery, etc. in that location.

    a) At Nava they started an eco-plantation and for this they have borne the entire expense, and the securities for this facility are provided by the organization.

    b) They frequently visit hospitals and provide patients with medicines and health drinks free of cost.

    c) They also arrange different types of camps for hepatitis vaccines in different locations throughout the country and provide people with free injections and medicines.

    They also have different milk collection centers at different sites where their plants are located, for example, at Nava and Rajamoondri, where their veterinary doctors provide free of cost maintenance and guidance to farmers regarding cattle rearing/caring and keeping so that cattle will provide good quality milk. And expenses related to cleaning, protecting and keeping the cattle are provided by SBCH free of cost.

Corporate HR people mainly make policies and give suggestions regarding the above practices.

The key result areas of the Corporate HR at SBCH are as follows:

■ Recruitment – Corporate HR feels that recruitment of the right person is a big challenge for the organization because SBCH believes that they are going to be the future building blocks of the organization.
■ Retention – Corporate HR people feel that retention of the right employee is also one of the key functions of the Corporate HR because they define the way in which any organization works and the effectiveness of any organization depends on good and the right people. For retention they are the leaders in terms of remuneration in the fast-moving consumer goods (FMCG) sector, and they have a very good organizational culture in terms of career growth opportunities, and so retention rate is very high in SBCH.
■ Growth opportunities – Identification of performance, recognition and rewarding performance makes people grow in the organization, which is also one of the key areas of the Corporate HR.

1. The relationship of the Corporate HR with the departments is also very good, and they also have cross-functional teams in the organization for various purposes to work effectively to achieve organizational goals. In this regard, the main policies are decided by the Corporate HR so that the different departments can associate with each other and work closely to achieve organizational goals.
2. The unit HR people do the main work regarding strategic manpower planning and here Corporate HR plays an advisory role.

3. Corporate HR plays a vital role as the business partner where they bring a unique people-oriented perspective to the corporate strategy formation and implementation. And in this regard, they formulate policies and practices such that every department acts in close coordination with each other to achieve the business objective.

4. Corporate HR plays a proactive role achieving the organization objective by building a future talent pool by training the relevant people with the relevant tools.

5. Regarding employee advocacy, they believe that they are the best in this regard by caring for different aspects of the employees and providing them with growth opportunities.

6. The corporate HR plays a role in the formulation of policies and the implementation of policies with regard to bringing in the required change in the organization.

7. The corporate HR plays an important role in the recruitment and selection of management trainees and people of a certain organizational hierarchy because they think that it is necessary to have a uniform level of talent pool in the organization and the unit HR managers take care of the rest.

8. There is a separate training and development department at the corporate head office which decides on the basis of the nature of training required and the type of training to be given to the required people or the team. One unique feature in this regard is that they have a separate training and development department for salespersons, which is taken care of by the corporate training and development department. The Corporate HR mainly assists them with different types of ideas. They also use the SmithKline Academy for training the required people.

9. One important aspect is that they concentrate on the generation of ideas within the organization for which they select the relevant ideas and recognize and reward good ideas; as part of this policy, employees have to submit

their ideas and they get an instant gift token from their supervisor, and if the idea is good then they are implemented for day-to-day activities.

10. Trade unions: SBCH has very good relations with trade unions, and they empower trade unions for various practices.

11. The transforming culture: Corporate HR also plays a vital part in this; for example when they shifted their corporate office from Delhi to Gurgaon, not a single employee left the organization, which was only due to the good culture promoted by the Corporate HR people which helps in retention of the employees and the employers in turn help the employees to adapt to the new corporate culture.

12. Career growth and development: Corporate HR also plays a vital role and for this they have policies so that people from one department can shift to other departments, for example people from HR can shift to the marketing or logistics department and can grow in terms of career in that department.

Competencies required for the Corporate HR people:

- Empathy
- Good understanding of the business and business processes
- Flexible in dealing with people and implementing ideas
- Learning attitude

Notes Based on Discussions with Mr. Roy Chowdhary of Baxter

Mr. Roy Chowdhary is currently working with Baxter as Head HR (India)

1. The Corporate HR is essential to bring about transparency across the organization so that there can be uniformity in policies and practices in the organization and everyone

feel equally committed and dedicated to achieve organizational goals and in this way the Corporate HR helps the organization to become a center of excellence. The Corporate HR can be a center of excellence only through providing innovative ideas and concepts and by coming up with new plans to provide an edge to the organization in a business environment.

2. The Corporate HR should design the HR policies and link the policy to the business objective.
3. The Corporate HR should work hand in hand with the finance department in designing the budget for the organization.
4. The Corporate HR bridges the gap of what is at the present and what is to be achieved and how it is to be achieved.
5. The Corporate HR is able to bridge the gap between the employee and the employer through performance appraisal, training and development and consultation sessions which helps in sorting out problems.
6. The Corporate HR brings the supervisor and the subordinate on the same platform.
7. In Baxter they have a standard training program. According to the training needs and requirements, they send their employees abroad for training and development. The Corporate HR helps in the process of cultural awareness by sending the people abroad and by keeping in touch with employees worldwide through online communication channels.
8. The Corporate HR is a facilitator and consultant to the unit and divisional HR and provides value addition to them.

In Baxter they don't have a unit and divisional HR. They are in the process of developing a manufacturing plant at Manesar. They are divided into four regions, there Corporate HR's role is to select the right person for those particular regions and also the regional guys are the main strength. According to the Corporate HR at Baxter, the role is to develop the company's philosophy across the unit and division, and to align the different units.

1. In terms of fulfilling governmental and societal obligations, Baxter is into the manufacturing of medical equipment, which are used in dialysis, renal transplants, angioplasty and also life-saving drugs. In this context they focus on better quality products and help people in leading a healthier life. The good quality of these drugs and equipments is the biggest governmental and societal obligation.

2. Business strategist/business partner: The Corporate HR acts as a business partner with different departments like Bioscience, finance, marketing and renal. HR works with the finance department in preparing the budget for the organization.

3. Recruitment and selection: The HR department does the recruitment through external placement agencies, industrial contacts and personal contacts.

4. Compensation and benefits: In Baxter the key HR issue like compensation and benefit is based on individual performance, role and responsibility of the individual.

5. Cultural awareness and transforming culture: Being a multinational company, Baxter provides better opportunities for interaction with different people and provides an environment for employees to get acquainted with different cultures . In this process, they are connected through the Internet so employees are able to interact their colleagues in India as well as abroad and they are aware of the different cultures which helps in employees' adaptability to different cultures.

6. Retention of quality manpower: In Baxter, people believe in the transparency of the system, for which they have a flat structure. They have a very good compensation package and they also empower the

employees' roles and responsibilities. They also do surveys to measure employee satisfaction and employees' involvement to retain their employees.

7. In terms of key result areas of the Corporate HR, they emphasize on uniformity in the performance management system and the development of key resources across units in the organization. The Corporate HR also looks into the training and development program and compensation in addition to providing guidance to the employee.

Communicating the organization's philosophy, objective and vision is to be reflected in a very effective manner. Competencies required in the Corporate HR:

1. Good communication skills	7. Logical ability
2. Good listener	8. Role model
3. Good interpersonal skills	9. Empathetic
4. Problem solving attitude	10. Helpful
5. Good knowledge of HR practices	11. Business acumen
6. Rational presentation skills	12. Generous

Notes Based on Discussions with the HR Head of Samtel

■ First of all, the most important aspect is that the need and importance of the Corporate HR should be recognized and felt by the organization from within, i.e., to coordinate and align all people-related issues from all the departments and units of the organization. In any organization production, marketing, and finances are not the only reality, because these functions are done by people, and so the most important asset for any organization is their human resource. If human resources are developed, then through them the organization will also develop. So the Corporate HR helps the organization in achieving the long-term goals of the organization by aligning the short-term operational goals of the organization through the development of the people of the organization as a whole. There are two aspects of the truth: one is tangible which people can understand and the other is intangible which people cannot understand. So the Corporate HR helps the organization to achieve the tangible benefits through the intangible people-related aspects

The objectives of the Corporate HR should be:

■ To help the organization in the formulation and achievement of its strategy
■ To think, visualize, conceptualize and design the human resource aspect of the organization
■ To be proactive in building and developing the human resource aspect of the organization according to the business strategy and the changes in the business environment

The benefits of the Corporate HR are:

■ It helps the organization to achieve the business results through the development and better utilization of the human resources of the organization.
■ It helps the organization as a lever to achieve the business results through different ways like providing training and development, proper communication, motivation and change in culture, etc. (Figure 6.3.)
■ It helps the organization to be best in its work culture by building the kind of environment in which people can excel in their job performance.

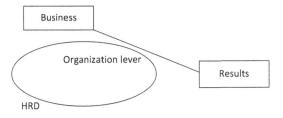

Figure 6.3   Relationship of strategic HRM with business performance.

Organizational mission of the corporate HR

- The role of the Corporate HR should be to provide an overall organization mission whereas the unit HR should provide know-how on the routines and operational jobs. The Corporate HR does the planning and provides value addition to the operational job and helps in achieving the organizational objective by aligning all the operational aspects of the job to the overall organizational mission.

- The role of the Corporate HR on governmental and societal obligations is that it should institute some kind of processes and thought about what the organization does for the individual, community and society, which can be reflected in the top management's process, and the Corporate HR should be able to convince the top management by its performance and competencies regarding governmental and societal obligations so that the top management can also join in and can include this in its organizational policies and practices.

- The role of the Corporate HR in key result areas of the organization is that first the organization should do strategic planning and then achieve that through yearly planning; then on the basis of that planning, unit and departmental level key result areas should be fixed and to support all this individual key result areas should be fixed.

The key result areas of the Corporate HR are listed below.

The Corporate HR should be a strategic thinker who should:

- Add value to the whole business
- Be master of all business activities
- Know all the business processes
- Be aware of business tools
- Acknowledge and accept the HR concerns of the different departments and units
- Be well-equipped with all the required HR knowledge
- Know the pulse of the business
- Know the internal and external business environment and business pressure
- Provide strategic ideas

- The role of the Corporate HR should be interrelated with the different departments to achieve the desired business results. In an organization, the marketing department knows the grip and pulse of the business in the current business environment, whereas the finance department provides the information regarding the financial performance of the organization, the financial status and need of the organization and happenings in the share market in terms of shareholder values and market values and collaborates all the departmental units' financial needs, whereas the production department provides the information regarding the production needs and relative requirements and finally the Corporate HR should be able to cement all the HR functions of the organization and should help the organization in all the HR needs of the organization like legal requirements, compensation design, manpower planning for the organization to use the human resource of the organization in the most effective way, and for all this the Corporate HR executive must have the knowledge of economics, psychology, law, personnel etc.

According to HR Head of Samtel, other departments like production, marketing and finance generate money for the organization but HR in the short term generally does not generate money but helps the organization in the long term to achieve the business objectives and develop the organizational human resources of the organization.

1. The role of Corporate HR in strategic manpower planning should be such that it will utilize the right number and the right kind of person with the required competencies to achieve the organizational objectives.
2. The Corporate HR should act as a business partner to the top management. It should build such an environment and implement such policies and practices where people can excel in their performance to achieve the business objectives.
3. The role of the Corporate HR should be proactive such that it identifies the future needs of the organization and the required competencies and should provide appropriate training and development to the individual according to the business needs. For this the Corporate HR should first help the top management in planning the business plan and the required competencies to achieve the business objectives; then the training and development should be planned and implemented for the required process, and so in this regard the Corporate HR should act as an architect.
4. As an employee, the advocacy role of Corporate HR is to ensure employability of the people in an appropriate way and marketability of the HR function to the top management so that employees can feel proud to associate with the organization, for which the Corporate HR should create the kind of culture that will help the employees in their performance.

5. The role of the Corporate HR as a change agent is very important in bringing about the change in the organization through people according to the business needs and the changing business environment through implementation of various policies and practices. So the Corporate HR must have a sense of mission, should stand for a bigger cause, submerge others' ego and have genuine concern for others. They should also provide training and development, a change in culture and other policies to bring about a change in the organization according to the business needs.

6. The role of the Corporate HR in recruitment and selection is to lay down the necessary assessment methods and master the implementation of the assessment methods for the individual, group and organization and should be able to diagnose self-appraisals to select the right person for the organization.

7. The role of the Corporate HR as a facilitator is to facilitate different departments and units to deal with people-related issues in a proper way and help them to implement the organizational objectives by aligning the short-term objectives with the long-term objectives of the organization through the people of the organization.

8. Today the role of the Corporate HR is not only a problem solver but also a consultant which is very important because in today's business environment the organization has to be proactive in identifying the needs of the organization and should provide appropriate suggestions to deal with the situation and have an edge over other organizations in that environment through its people.

9. The role of the Corporate HR in compensation and benefits is not only to pay according to the labor law and economics but also should be such that it can motivate the employees and fulfill their needs.

10. The role of the Corporate HR in retention should be such that it should retain the right person for the organization; people who are not fit for the organization should leave the organization and fresh talent and ideas should keep coming into the organization.
11. The role of the Corporate HR in total quality management is to help the employees to develop in the future course of their professional lives.
12. The role of the Corporate HR with respect to performance development and growth is that it should devise such policies and practices that it helps the employee regarding clarity of life and purpose as what he is doing is a smaller part of the overall mission of his life, so it should help the employees in their career development with the organizational development.
13. The role of the Corporate HR for performance management development is that it should provide steps that support the organization's system and bring in the required competencies in the employee.
14. The role of the Corporate HR in transforming the culture is that first it should devise the policies of how this will happen in the organization, and then should provide the necessary steps for this.

The competencies required in Corporate HR people are:

• Centrality	• Diplomacy
• Institution builder	• Empathy
• Change agent	• High self-esteem
• Self-esteem	• Sense of autonomy
• Genuine concern for others	• Listening ability
• Master in HR knowledge	• Knowledge and awareness
• Motivator – Expert in influencing the business	

Bibliography

Delaney, J. T. & Huselid, M. A. 1996. The impact of human resource management practices on perceptions of organizational performance. *Academy of Management Journal*, 39: 949–969.

Fombrun, C. J., Tichy, N. M. & Devanna, M.A. 1984. *Strategic Human Resource Management*. New York, NY: Wiley.

Gratton, L., Hailey, V., Stiles, P. & Truss, C. 1999. *Strategic Human Resource Management*. Oxford: Oxford University Press.

Armstrong, M. 2014. *Armstrong's Handbook of Human Resource Management Practice*. London: Kogan Page.

LaMarco, N. 2018. What are HRM strategies? https://smallbusiness.chron.com/hrm-strategies-59260.html.

Mohanasundaram, V. Strategic human resource management – introduction. https://www.scribd.com/presentation/235421168/shrm-1.

Perez, V. M. 2013. Does HRM generate ambidextrous employees for ambidextrous learning? The moderating role of management support. *XXIII Congreso Nacional de Acede Septiembre de 2013*, Malaga, 1–30.

Purcell, J. 1989. The impact of corporate strategy on human resource management. In: J Storey (Ed.), *New Perspectives on Human Resource Management*. London: Routledge.

Whittington, Richard. 2000. *What is Strategy and Does it Matter?* 2nd Ed. Boston, MA: Cengage Learning.

Chapter 7

Strategies for Improving Organizational Effectiveness

Corporate HR at the Heart of the Business

Performance Management

The organization can improve the performance of its employees through the implementation of the performance management process, which has as its central agenda the demonstration of individual expertise to improve the company's bottom line results, and it should enable employees to combine knowledge with business acumen and cultural sensitivity and to understand the complex ramifications of the subject in their own environment. This process improves the overall growth of the organization, and can increase teamwork, cooperation, collaboration and customer service.

Organizational Development

For organizational development it is necessary that there is a visible top management which provides vision to the organization, whereas the middle management inspires and encourages people and enables them to change. It is also essential that teamwork is encouraged in the organization, and the contribution of the team should provide value addition to the organization. High energy people will make the organization progress toward achieving its vision.

Employee Development

Employee development should be planned and managed to optimize the needs of the organization and the preference of the individual, so that employees can change jobs within the organization when the opportunity arises. This is important because individuals want to use their complete range of skills and talent and to excel in whatever they do. So, consideration of employee development is very important for the organization, taking into account the need of the organization.

Employee Relation

The business environment in which employee–employer relations exists is important, and it is necessary to make this environment healthy so that the needs of both the employee and employer are satisfied.

Corporate HR should have the competency to implement the organization's policies and practices in an effective way in the existing business environment, and it is also important that they must have proper technology like computerized systems so that strategic contributions can be made to the developmental agenda.

The results of all these organizational developments are the following:

- Win-Win situation for both the employee and employer
- Bottom line results for the organization
- Required competency development in employees within the organization

So in this way the Corporate HR by being at the heart of the organization makes the organization excel in the existing business environment. HR being a specialized body of knowledge includes the study of many fields like sociology, economics, law, personnel etc., which helps Corporate HR in dealing with people through many dimensions and angles, and it also helps employees to have a wide perception of the views regarding organizational policies and practices. This enables transparency across the organization so that there can be uniformity in policies and practices of the organization, and it can help employees in taking uniform decisions that are aligned with the organization's policies.

Corporate HR acts as the central agency to coordinate the people-related issues of all the departments and units in an effective way so that everyone feels equally committed to the organizational goal. Therefore, it is crucial for Corporate HR to be innovative, creative, customer focused and act according to the changes happening in the business environment.

The importance of Corporate HR should be felt within the organization by the different departments and units. It should be the center of excellence through innovative and new practices, policies, ideas, concepts and plans.

Corporate HR should be able to:

- Formulate HR strategies and initiatives in alignment with the business strategy
- Manage processes intelligently and efficiently
- Maximize employee contribution and commitment
- Create the environment for constant change

Corporate HR should act according to organizational goals and should always add value to the organization through its function, and so it must be clear about its objective on what course of action should be taken to add value. A very good example of how clarity of objective is important for any course of action is found in Lewis Carroll's book *Alice's Adventure in Wonderland* when Alice talks to the Cheshire cat who shows that there Alice lacks clarity of purpose, and the conversation goes like this:

Alice: Would you tell me please, which way I ought to go from here?
Cheshire cat: That depends a good deal on where you want to get to.
Alice: I do not much care where.
Cheshire cat: Then it does not matter which way you go.

This example illustrates that you should be clear about your objective and how you are going to achieve it otherwise you will end up nowhere; hence Corporate HR should be clear about its purpose of how it will help the organization in achieving its business objective. For this Corporate HR should not only know the science of the different HR processes and practices but also the art of implementing those ideas effectively through people. Whenever any organization works in any business environment, it sets both short-term and long-term goals and objectives for the organization, and generally production, sales, marketing and finance helps the organization to achieve the short-term goals by utilizing the current resources of the organization but Corporate HR helps the organization to achieve the long-term goals developing the human resource of the organization.

Corporate HR is bridges the gap between the organization's present performance and its desired state of performance by designing and implementing the organization's policies and practices.

The objectives of Corporate HR should be:

■ To think, visualize, conceptualize and design the HR practices of the organization
■ To proactively build and develop the HR practices of the organization according to the business objective and the business environment
■ To evolve a Corporate HR policy that would seek to achieve both business goals as well as employee needs
■ To further improve the current HR practices by identifying various areas of improvements in the system
■ To ensure the uniform implementation of all the HR policies and practices across all locations of the organization
■ To play a strategic role in the organization and help the organization in to achieve the business objectives strategically.

Benefits of Corporate HR

■ Corporate HR promotes the right kind of culture, value and vision to achieve the organizational objective.
■ Corporate HR standardizes the form of policies and practices so that every new member in the organization should talk one language and feel equally committed and dedicated to the organization.
■ Corporate HR coordinates all the HR activities of the organization to achieve the goal.
■ Corporate HR works toward achievement of the business results through different tools, e.g. training and development, communication, motivation and culture change, etc.
■ Corporate HR benchmarks its current HR practices with the best HR practices of organizations worldwide so that:

■ there can be improvements in current HR practices
■ competition can be faced by improving the overall functioning of the organization

- there is uniformity and equal treatment
- there is employee development for achieving business results
- competencies can be built building to face challenges
- employee satisfaction can be increased thereby ensuring high productivity
- the desired level of relationship (ownership and sense of belongingness) and communication is built in the organization.

Roles of Corporate HR

Role of Corporate HR in Relation to Unit HR/Divisional HR

Corporate HR plays a very important role in aligning the activities of the divisional HR and the unit HR through its policies and practices. As unit HR people act in different plant so they know the reality of human resource process at the plant level and can give the information regarding how these things are operating at the plant level to the Corporate HR then the Corporate HR sees that these processes are operating at the desired way or not. If not, then whether these functions should be done in some other way. For this both the doer and the planner of the HR processes should sit together and plan the desired HR function which can bring effectiveness in the organization then unit HR implements the suggested plan which can be implemented at unit level or not and what are the positive and negative outcomes of it and what other changes are required to implement the plan effectively.

Some Role of Corporate HR is to plan and provide the unit HR with a wider vision and perspective to achieve the organizational goals rather than doing routine jobs. Corporate HR is a facilitator and consultant to the unit HR and should provide a common focus to the unit and Divisional HR and also business partner to top management in helping the organization to achieve its objective by planning and implementing the people aspect of the business. Corporate HR also plays the advisory role and should guide unit and divisional HR to implement its plans in a proper and effective way by providing the overall mission of the organization.

The Relationship of Corporate HR with Different Departments

Role of Corporate HR in relation with different departments is of complementary nature like the marketing department knows the grip and pulse of the existing business environment, whereas the finance department provides the perception of the individual regarding financial status and need of the organization and also the happening in the share market in terms of shareholders value, market values and collaborating all the departments units and financial needs. Finally, Corporate HR cements all the needs like legal requirements, compensation, future manpower planning etc. to use the human resource of an organization in the most effective way. Corporate HR also involves other departments in policy making so that they associate with each other and work closely to achieve organizational goals. Corporate HR builds coherence, unity and consensus among the different departments. In terms of organizational culture and organizational objectives, Corporate HR uses various methods to be in touch with the employees and update them with the future course of action, such as communicating through the internet and newsletters and meeting employees at regular intervals. Here Corporate HR functions as a specialist service department concerned with the formulation and introduction of schemes, maintaining parity in the implementation of the schemes and modifying and proposing new schemes. Corporate HR would need to identify the problems faced by other departments and they should come up with an innovative and creative approach to solve these problems, especially problems related to organizational structure; work allocation and design; and attracting, retaining and managing people. The relationship of the Corporate HR with the different departments is very sensitive in nature and so they must try to increase the level of enthusiasm and efficiency for the successful accomplishment of organizational objectives.

Governmental and Societal Obligations of Corporate HR

This question of how Corporate HR fulfills its governmental and societal obligations arises at a point of time when we think about how far we have come (either in the right or wrong direction) from the early days of independence when there was not only a belief but a commitment to create a society.

Any organization can fulfill societal and governmental obligations by fulfilling the responsibilities of the business toward:

■ Itself
■ Its customers
■ Its workers
■ Its shareholders
■ The community
■ The country

An organization plays multiple societal and governmental roles in its business of earning profit, effective functioning, and making different types of tax payments, and through these roles it can contribute to the development of the society. One of the prime motives of any organization is to satisfy its customers through its products and services, and for this it is necessary that the internal customer of the organization, that is the employees, are satisfied. When the business earns

profits there is a constant return to the shareholders; the organization thus should also take care of the community in which
it is working and serve the country through different welfare
activities, especially for the weaker sections of society as and
when the need arises.

In this context, an example of a massive welfare program
was Operation Flood (Amul), which produced plenty of opportunity for employment. This initiative fulfilled both societal and
governmental obligations. Actually it is a matter of concern of
how much we think about the government and society. We
visited many places and received different views on this. Now
in this context what we think about the role of Corporate HR
is that it should institute some kind of process and also something for the individual, community and society, which can
be deflected in the top management. Corporate HR should be
able to convince the top management by its performance and
competencies regarding both obligations. So that the concern
percolates till the bottom through the top management itself.
Corporate HR's role is to provide suggestions regarding obligations and try to implement it. In the present era, we have to
think about how we can meet the challenges of unemploy-
ment, tax payment, illiteracy, bad condition of villages and poor
health, etc. The Corporate HR is well placed in the position of
providing suggestions to such community issues and in making
relevant policies, thereby accomplishing their role in fulfilling
these obligations. If an organization shows concern toward the
government and the society, it holds its head proudly not only
for achieving organizational goals but also for its commitment to
justice and equity, which is the real success of the organization.

Role of Corporate HR in Strategic Manpower Planning

By the way of human resource strategies, the organization
plans to utilize its human resources, develop them and provide
them opportunities and better working conditions, so that the

maximum utilization of human resources is ensured. Strategic human resource planning is planning of the human resources of the organization in alignment with the organization strategy and business need of the organization, that is ensuring that it has the right number of people and the right kind of people at the right places at the right time doing the work for which they are economically most useful. The unit HR people and the different departmental heads know the actual status of employees' performance based on which they suggest to the Corporate HR on how strategic manpower should be planned according to the needs of the different units and the forecasted developments in order to achieve the objectives of the organization. Here Corporate HR mainly does the overall manpower planning and plays an advisory role. This basically includes organizational capability and gap identification, external and internal work climate assessment and people strategy formulation and implementation.

Role of Corporate HR as a Business Partner

One of the most important roles of the Corporate HR is to be a business partner of an organization, and therefore it should coordinate with the top management of the other departments so that it can help the organization in the formulation of business strategies regarding the human resources of the organization and help the top management to implement these strategies through better utilization of the human resources of the overall benefit of the organization.

So as a business partner it participates in the strategy formulation process and develops possible solutions to challenges that the organization may face, thus leading the business to competitive success.

Corporate HR in a Proactive Role

In today's turbulent and unpredictable business environment due to the changing technology, increasing globalization, continuous cost containment, increasing speed in the market, the growing importance of knowledge capital and the increasing rate and magnitude of change.

The role of Corporate HR is not to do only routine jobs but to act proactively so that through proper utilization and training and development of employees the organization can achieve a competitive advantage over its competitors. Therefore, the Corporate HR has to be proactive in finding what competencies are required in employees and should plan and suggest appropriate training methods to make the employees competent. The training needs identification is done by the different departmental heads and unit the HR person, and then the Corporate HR does the planning of the training while the implementation is done by the unit HR person. The employee to be trained should be informed accordingly 1 or 2 months prior and should be asked to be ready for the training program with required behavior, knowledge, skill and attitude.

This process can help the organization in the following ways:

- Reduce time between learning and application
- Focus on the present and future
- Can reduce cost
- Can increase organizational commitment
- Can increase organizational learning
- Concentrate both on the results or outcomes and processes

Role of Corporate HR as an Employee Advocate

The role of Corporate HR as an employee advocate is very important because in today's dynamic business scenario human resources are such a delicate commodity that proper and full attention should be given to the organization's human resources. The Corporate HR has to address every problem of the employees and try to solve these issues with appropriate policies and practices. Corporate HR, from time to time, should convey the demands and needs of the employees to the top management so that employees feel satisfied and properly cared for. Corporate HR should also formulate policies and practices such that it acts as an employee advocate.

Role of Corporate HR as a Change Agent

Corporate HR should play the following roles as a change agent:

- *Process Trainer*: They can suggest or provide training to employees explaining how the change process works, including definitions of purpose, diagnosis, problem solving and solutions.
- *Catalyst*: They anticipate and identify the organization's needs for change, and they also recognize the status quo and ensure that the change is satisfactory.
- *Information links*: They link the necessary resources together – including people, processes, and equipment – to accomplish the firm's objective.
- *Team leader or facilitator*: They have a solid grasp of the current organizational practices as well as of the organizational mission, goals and objectives, and as a change agent they must be aware of the organizational culture as it is the medium by which change is brought about in the organization.

To be an effective and successful change agent, they must possess certain personal characteristics. First, they must have the ability to gain and understand information about the market, competition and internal conditions of the business. Second, they must garner participation throughout the organization. Third, they must show perseverance in the face of the resistance they are sure to encounter during the change effort. Fourth, they must have a vision. Long-term change efforts lacking vision also usually lacks direction or focus. Fifth, change leaders must possess the proven ability to engineer change. Finally, they should exude a positive attitude and enjoy planning, analyzing, implementing and evaluating changes.

So, as a change agent Corporate HR should ask the following questions:

- What business needs require a change in the HR function?
- What changes are needed in the HR function?
- What are the changes needed in each HR functional area?
- How should the change be communicated?
- How will the results be measured?

Role of Corporate HR in Transforming the Culture and Creating Cultural Awareness

The word culture means:

> Culture is a pattern of basic assumption – invented discovered or developed by a given organization as it learns to cope with its problems of external adaptation and internal integration that has worked well enough to be considered valid and therefore to be taught to new members as the correct way to perceive, think, and feel in relations to those problems.

The Corporate HR's job in terms of culture building starts from the day a person joins the organization. The Corporate HR studies the working habits, practices and experiences of the people in the organization and then they do a survey, and on the basis of the outcome of this survey Corporate HR develops on the necessary areas of concern because the work culture of an organization is very much related to the organization's objective. Culture indicates work culture, which differs between countries, and for employees to cope up with the work culture Corporate HR should provide adequate opportunities for interaction with different people so that employees get aquatinted with different cultures. Today, with the advancement of information technology (NET, LAN etc.), this has become quite easy.

So Corporate HR should devise the appropriate policies to build a good organizational culture, which requires the following necessary steps

Measures for Developing a Good Organizational Culture

- Always use compliments and appreciation openly and widely to raise the morale of the employees when they do a good job.
- Always trust your employees.
- Stop favoritism in the organization.
- Freedom of expression should be encouraged.
- Believe in an open culture.
- Respect the right to speak.

In this way Corporate HR plays a very important role in building the work culture in the organization.

Role of Corporate HR in Recruitment and Selection

Recruitment is the process of generating a list of applicants for a specific job position, and selection refers to the process of offering the jobs to one or more applicants.

The role of Corporate HR in this regard is to plan the process of selection of the candidates and to set the selected candidates with the required competencies in the appropriate job positions so that a uniform pool of candidates with the right kind of competencies that are in alignment with the corporate culture, policies and practices join the organization's workforce and foster the organization's growth.

Therefore Corporate HR should play an active role in recruitment and selection so that the right kind and the right number of employees are recruited in the organization.

Role of Corporate HR in Career Development and Growth

Individual career development focuses on assisting individuals to identify their major career goals and determine what needs to be done to achieve these goals. Career development involves the development of an effective and successful long-term career of personnel within the organization. Corporate HR should formulate the policies to ensure individual career development in the organization with adequate employee training and management development efforts. The most important factor to be considered in this regard is that the career development policies should look toward developing people competencies for the long-term needs of the organization and be capable of dealing with the dynamic changes in the business environment while matching individual abilities and aspirations with the needs of the organization.

So Corporate HR should formulate policies which ensure that:

■ The needed talent will be available
■ The organization's ability to attract and remain high-talent personnel is improved
■ Minorities and women get opportunities for growth and development
■ Reduce employee frustration

Role of Corporate HR in Retention of Employees

It is very important for any organization to retain its employees who have the right kind of attitude, behavior, knowledge and skill so that the organization can ensure growth through these employees and also make sure that the desired talent pool retained in the organization works to build an organization capable of handling any challenge in the changing business environment.

Retention mainly depends on the type of industry and the type of employee, taking into account the needs of the organization.

For the retention of employees, Corporate HR can formulate different types of plans and policies. These may be of the following types:

- Good compensation package
- Good organizational culture and management practices
- Good growth opportunities
- Good learning opportunities.

Role of Corporate HR in Employee Compensation and Benefits

The role of Corporate HR is very important for structuring employee compensation and benefits, and it depends on the:

- Cost of living
- Productivity
- Prevailing business trends in compensation packages
- Ability to pay
- Company's compensation policy

People have different needs according to their age, financial and family position, attitude and lifestyle. Usually younger employees tend to favor benefits that can be frequent or of immediate use, such as vacation days, holiday packages and flexible working hours, whereas older employees tend to be security conscious, preferring life insurance and retirement-related benefits.

So Corporate HR should identify the need of the employee and make compensation and benefits package, which will fulfill both the employees and organizational objective.

Role of Corporate HR in Trade Union Relations

As trade unions generally operate at different units, the unit HR managers know the working and the activities of the trade unions and are aware of the real picture of the situation at the time of any dispute. In such cases the Corporate HR may either delegate its authority to the unit HR managers to deal with the situation or may play an advisory role and provide suggestions on how to deal with the situation effectively.

Corporate HR can also involve trade unions in the formulation and implementation of policies to achieve the organizational objective. In this way trade unions can also be engaged in the development of the organization and empowered to contribute to the achievement of organizational goals and will not involve in unnecessary disputes but work toward the development and growth of the organization.

Role of Corporate HR in Total Quality Management

Total quality management (TQM) is a people-focused management system that aims at the continual increase of customer satisfaction at low cost. It is a total system approach and an integral part of a high-level strategy. It works horizontally across the functions and departments, involving all employees, top to bottom, and extends backwards and forwards to include the supply chain and customer chain. It is the roof or super structure of four organizational subsystems within which the actual work for any organization takes place. The four subsystems are:

- Management subsystem
- Social subsystem
- Technical subsystem
- Education subsystem.

Deming defined the concept of a social subsystem that as "the people work in a system, the job of a manager is to work on the system to improve it continuously with their help." So that the following can be achieved in an organization:

- Organization norms, role responsibility, sociopsychological relations, expectations can be defined.
- Status and power relationships between individual members and among groups can be established.
- Work committee, competition, cooperation, motivation, creativity, innovative behavior and teamwork can be established.

Here the responsibility lies with the individual working for the organization.

Juan recommends the concept of a technical subsystem where the flow of work through the organization is necessary as it includes all the tools and machinery; the focus on quality and the quantification of quality is necessary for an organization because only when quality can be measured then it can be discussed and improved upon.

Educational subsystem: It focuses on creating and developing a global learning organization to continuously expanding the knowledge horizons of the stakeholders to gain a competitive advantage.

Management subsystem deals with:

- The organization design, polices, pattern of authority and budgetary control
- Mission, vision and goal of the institution
- Administrative activities: Planning, organization, designing, coordinating and controlling organizational activities.

So these subsystems are the top layer of the theoretical part of TQM.

The four pillars of quality provide the strategic direction, which are:

- Customer satisfaction
- Continuous improvement
- Speaking with the facts
- Respect for the people

The four foundations are:

- Strategy management: It is the process of strategic plan implementation, evaluation and control to develop the competitive advantage and to ensure a favorable future for the organization.
- Process management: It is the coordination and implementation of measured, streamlined and controlled processes to continuously improve operations.
- Project management: It is the implementation and control of a single, nonrecurring event that activates organizational change through structured phases and specified outcomes and requires teamwork for successful competition.
- Performance management: It is the implementation and control of respectful regard for oneself and others in line with total quality strategies, processes and projects.

Then four cornerstones of total quality management are:

- *Strategic planning*: It is the process of environmental analysis and strategy formulation to determine an organization's future directional stability.
- *Process planning*: It is the step which ensures that all key processes work in harmony with the mission and meet the needs and expectations of the constituents or customers by maximizing operational effectiveness.
- *Project planning*: It is the establishment of a system to effectively plan, organize, implement and control all the activities needed for the successful completion of project initiatives.
- *Performance planning*: It is the process that provides all employees with the means to implement continuous improvements in processes and systems through the completion of individual tasks and activities. The mortar deployed between the joints of the roof, the pillars, the foundation and the cornerstones is the interactive process of participation and feedback that builds a sense of ownership and commitment so that the structure of total quality is built both domestically and internationally.

Finally, the ethical work culture of an organization determines whether a house becomes a home – a place where respect, cooperation, trust, care, justice and high performance prevails so that the organization becomes a center of excellence and can face competition.

World over, TQM is a proven tool/way of management which helps the firm in becoming a world-class organization. TQM provides a platform for balancing the attitude of the employees, aligning with the organizational vision both in self-life and work-life. The journey of implementing TQM is about changing the existing work culture and management style to a TQM culture, which means changing the mindset and practices of people, i.e., bringing about a paradigm shift. Corporate

HR has the a major and primary role next to that of the top management in the culture change process. We suggest that apart from implementing the "change process," Corporate HR people should set an example. They should first do it and then show it. Sadly this is one of the areas neglected by change seekers and implementers, i.e. Corporate HR.

Competencies and Qualities Required for Corporate HR

Competency is an underlying characteristic of a person which enables them to deliver superior performance in a given job, role or situation in terms of knowledge, skill, behavior and attitude.

On the basis of our study, we suggest that the following are the competencies and qualities required for Corporate HR people:

- Flexibility regarding operations and leadership
- Knowledge of the overall business process
- Understanding of internal benchmarking procedures
- Knowledge and awareness of HR systems practiced worldwide
- Knowledge and awareness of the HR system
- Thorough knowledge of industrial and labor laws
- Good interpersonal skills
- Consensus building ability
- Presentation skills
- Good listener
- Learning attitude
- Genuine concern for others
- Helpful
- Empathetic
- Role model possessing a sense of autonomy
- Leadership quality

- Sensitive to human feelings
- Believe in action
- Analytical skills
- Reasoning ability
- High self-esteem
- Diplomatic
- Institution builder

Training and Development Process

The new age of business management has brought with it a plethora of challenges and opportunities. To survive in this environment, business strategies have to be constantly and rigorously analyzed and, if need be, modified too. The pace is both frightening and exciting.

With a focus on customer orientation, on the need for continuous development, on recognizing high achievement, on flexibility and responsiveness, companies are realizing this importance of employee training and development.

There is a continuous endeavor on the part of the top management to make their organization a learning origination.

Apollo Tyres Limited (ATL), an ISO9001 company, considers training to be an important and integral part of its business strategy and therefore regularly conducts internal or external training for its employees. It is one of the primary functions of HR. The ED&GP form is specifically meant to gather and collate the training needs of ATL's employees. The map of training and development process is discussed in the next section (Figure 7.1)

Role of Corporate HR in Training and Development

Time Is Not Lost in Hours, but in Minutes

To become world-class competitors, businesses must recognize the importance of the processes in its day-to-day life.

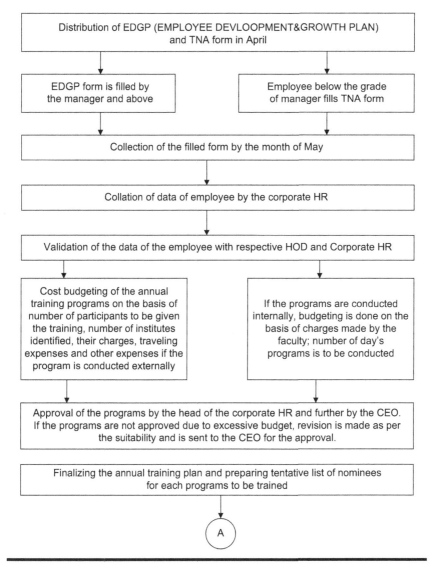

Figure 7.1   Strategies for improving organizational effectiveness.

These processes are the cutting edge of world-class competition. To understand the impact of these processes, we must have the ability to describe, quantify and analyze them. The first step in controlling these processes is to perform a Process Analysis, which is a tactical tool used to develop strategies to innovate and improve processes.

A process is a transformation of inputs such as people, materials, equipment, methods and environment into finished products through a series of value-added activities.

Before any process can be quantified, analyzed and subjected to continuous measurable improvement, the system must first be effectively described. The method for providing a structured description of the system is the process flowchart. There are six phases to performing the Process Analysis.

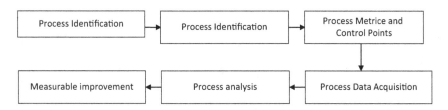

Continuous Improvement with Respect to Process Identification

Although there are dozens of activities that are performed in organizations, to implement continuous improvement we must select those activities that are critical to the mission and vision of the organization.

Implementing continuous improvements begins with the identification of the process. First, we must differentiate between the three types of processes: industrial, administrative and management.

Industrial processes are the processes that produce things. Processes such as repair and rebuilding are also industrial processes.

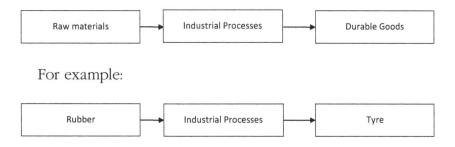

For example:

Management processes are structured techniques by which businesses and individuals make key decisions. This structured, quantifiable approach to decision making is based on fact-based decisions.

For example:

Administrative processes are the processes that customers (both internal and external) most frequently find quite frustrating. Administrative processes produce the paper, data and information that other processes use. These processes also include products that are used directly by the customers, such as medical reimbursements, housing loans, provident funds, etc.

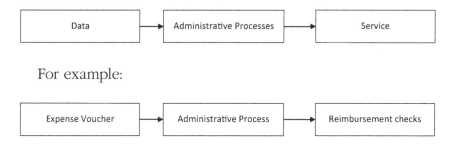

For example:

The identification process requires that we understand more than just the name and type of the process, so that we can make informed decision about which processes to manage. It is essential to:

a) Acquire and review all process documentation. Shortlist the Processes to be mapped.
b) Determine process ownership. Who has direct responsibility? What kind of process is it? Where does it begin and end, etc.?

Conclusion, Recommendation and Key Issues

This study carried out as part of the strategic HR project consisted of designing approaches to strategic HRM of the organization. It involved a detailed study of the different roles of Corporate HR and different HR processes, so that it can add value to the organization through its policies and practices. It gave an overview of each aspect of the role of Corporate HR and explained the different HR practices associated with it.

The role of strategic HR helps the organization deal with the different HR requirements of the organization by formulating and implementing different HR policies and practices from its position as business partner to the top management .

The research helped me to understand the basic role of Corporate HR and different HR processes, and my practical experiences of HR practices in organizations and my study on different Corporate HR practices have will be useful learning material and provide insightful comments for students and practicing professionals. I hope this research on the role of strategic human resource management will be a value addition for the corporate world.

Recommendation

1. Human resources strategy must be anchored to the business strategy.
2. Human resources management is not about programs, but rather, about relationships.
3. The HR department must be an agency that anticipates change and understands what is necessary to implement it
4. Although HR should be an advocate of employee interests, it must understand that business decisions need to be balanced over a range of factors that may conflict with one another.
5. The effectiveness of human resources depends on it remaining focused on issues rather than on personalities.

6. Human resource executives must accept that constant learning and skill enhancement are essential to their role as contributors to the business.

Changing Role of HR

In addition to the traditional functions performed by HR specialists, the role of HR professionals is undergoing a significant change to meet the organization's demands for improved quality, reduced costs and constant innovation. The HR role has extended to provide training and development to employees who are capable of responding to the changing priorities.

- 75% of the organizations surveyed have outlined a broad HR strategy.
- In 89% of the organizations surveyed the HR head is a member of the top management committee.
- 75% of the organizations surveyed have indicated that the human resource plan is nowadays becoming an integral part of the business plan.
- In 13 organizations, HR managers are responsible for organizational development.
- Sixteen of the surveyed organizations have indicated that their HR department oversees total quality management.
- Several organizations have adopted a system of manpower planning and forecasting. Manpower planning is the process through which organizations estimate the demand for manpower over a specified period.
- About 11 of the surveyed organizations have indicated that their HR department has undertaken culture-building initiatives among its employees. One of the participating organizations has introduced a Hajj program, which sponsors the pilgrimage of five employees each year to Mecca.
- 89% of the surveyed organizations have indicated that they have a well-documented HR policies and procedures manual.

- 72% of the surveyed organizations acknowledged that their HR policies have been properly communicated to all employees.
- At least 24 of the participating organizations have a well-established HR database, which integrates employee details and provides data on personal information, promotions, transfers, employee performance and development needs.
- About 27 of the participating organizations have indicated that the average spending on the human resources function is around 7% of their operating costs.

Key Issues

- Organizations should develop a well-articulated HR vision linked to the corporate vision. This should be the basis for evolving the HR strategy. The HR strategy should be shared with employees at all levels and in all functions. It needs to be backed by key action steps and plans. It is essential to translate the HR strategy of the organizations into specific quantifiable and measurable action plans.
- Organizations should appropriately communicate the human resources policies and procedures among its employees and promote its effective implementation.

Bibliography

Alchian, A. A. & Demsetz, H. 1972. Production, information costs, and economic organization. *American Economic Review*, 62(December): 777–795.

Armstrong, M. 2006. *A Handbook of Human Resource Management Practice*, 10th Ed. Cambridge: Cambridge University Press.

Armstrong, M. 2006. *Performance Management: Key Strategies and Practical Guidelines*, 3th Ed. London: Kogan Page Limited.

Armstrong, M. 2006. *Strategic Human Resource Management: A Guide to Action*, 3th Ed. London: Thomson-Shore, Inc.

Boxall, P. & Purcell, J. 2003.*Strategy and Human Resource Management.* Basingstoke and New York: Palgrave Macmillan.

Boxall, P., Purcell, J. & Wright, P. 2007. The Oxford handbook of "Human resource management". In: B. Gerhart (Ed.), *Modeling HRM and Performance Linkages*, 552–580. Oxford: Oxford University Press.

Boxall, P., Purcell, J. & Wright, P. 2007. The Oxford handbook of Human resource management. In: G. Latham, L. M. Sulsky & H. MacDonald (Eds.), *Performance Management*, 364–384. Oxford: Oxford University Press.

Boxall, P., Purcell, J. & Wright, P. 2007. The Oxford handbook of Human resource management. In: J. Purcell & N. Kinnie, *HRM and Business Performance*, 533–551. Oxford: Oxford University Press.

Brewster, C. et al. 2000.*Contemporary Issues in Human Resource Management: Gaining a Competitive Advantage.* Cape Town: Oxford University Press.

Brumbach, G. B. 1988. Some ideas, issues and predictions about performance management. *Public Personnel Management*, Winter, 387–402.

Campbell, J. P. 1999. The definition and measurement of performance in the new age. In: D. R. Ilgen & E. D. Pulakos (Eds.), *The Changing Nature of Performance. Implications for Staffing, Motivation, and Development*, 399–429. San Francisco, CA: Jossey-Bass.

Dyer, L. & Reeves, T. 1995. Human resource strategies and firm performance: What do we know and where do we need to go? *Paper presented at the 10th World Congress of the International Industrial Relations Association*, Washington, DC.

Guest, D. E. 1987. Human resource management and industrial relations. *Journal of Management Studies*, 24(5): 503–521.

Guest, D. E. 2011. Human resource management and performance: still searching for some answers. *Human Resource Management Journal*, 21(1): 3–13.

Hendry, C. & Pettigrew, A. 1990. Human resource management: An agenda for the 1990s. *International Journal of Human Resource Management*, 1: 17–43.

Holbeche, L. 2004. How to make work more meaningful. *Personnel Today*, 26.

Janssens, M. & Steyaert, C. 2009. HRM and performance: A plea for reflexivity in HRM studies. *Journal of Management Studies*, 46(1): 143–155.

Lance, C. E. 1994. Test of a latent structure of performance ratings derived from Wherry's (1952) theory of ratings. *Journal of Management*, 20: 757–771.

Lifson, K. A. 1953. Errors in time-study judgments of industrial work pace. *Psychological Monographs*, 67(355): 1–163.

Noe, R., Hollenbeck, J. R., Gerhart, B. & Wright, P. M. 2007. *Fundamentals of Human Resource Management*, 2nd Ed. Boston, MA: McGraw-Hill.

Pfeffer, J. 1998. Seven practices of successful organizations. *California Management Review*, 40(2): 96–124.

Purcell, J. 1999. High commitment management and the link with contingent workers: implications for strategic human resource management. *Research in Personnel and Human Resources Management*.

Rogers, E. W. & Wright, P. M. 1998. Measuring organizational performance in strategic human resource management: Problems, prospects, and performance information markets. *Human Resource Management Review*, 8(3): 311.

Ronan, W. W. & Prien, E. P. 1971. *Perspectives on the Measurement of Human Performance*. New York, NY: Appleton-Century-Crof.

Index

Printed in the United States
by Baker & Taylor Publisher Services